STREET FRENCH 1

D0973697

To order the accompanying cassette for

STREET FRENCH 1

See the coupon on the last page for details

STREET FRENCH 1

The Best of French Slang

David Burke

John Wiley & Sons, Inc.

New York • Chichester • Brisbane • Toronto • Singapore

Design and Production: Optima PrePress
Copy Editor: Dr. Ralph Baccash
Front Cover Illustration: Ty Semaka
Inside Illustrations: Ty Semaka

This publication is designed to provide accurate and authoritative information in regard to the subject matter covered. It is sold with the understanding that the publisher is not engaged in rendering legal, accounting, or other professional services. If legal advice or other expert assistance is required, the services of a competent professional person should be sought. FROM A DECLARATION OF PRINCIPLES JOINTLY ADOPTED BY A COMMITTEE OF THE AMERICAN BAR ASSOCIATION AND A COMMITTEE OF PUBLISHERS.

Copyright © 1996 by David Burke
Published by John Wiley & Sons, Inc.

All rights reserved. Published simultaneously in Canada.

Reproduction or translation of any part of this work beyond that permitted by section 107 or 108 of the 1976 United States Copyright Act without the permission of the copyright owner is unlawful. Requests for permission or further information should be addressed to the Permission Department, John Wiley & Sons.

Library of Congress Cataloging-in-Publication Data
Burke, David
Street French 1 : the best of French slang / David Burke.
p. cm.
Includes index.
ISBN 0-471-13898-3 (paper : alk. paper)
1. French language - Slang. 2. French language - Textbooks for foreign speakers - English. I. Title.
PC3739.B872 1996
448.3'421 - dc20 96-4202

Printed in the United States of America
10 9 8 7 6 5 4 3 2

This book is dedicated to my father.

ACKNOWLEDGMENTS

My special thanks to Jerri Simon Borack, whose inspiration was the catalyst for my interest in pursuing the French language; my family and friends in France for their unyielding help and patience in spending hours at a time going over the latest slang words and expressions with me: Mimi, Patrice, Carole, Christophe, Régis, Nélie, & Serge; Pascale Ledeur and Mark Maisonneuve for all their help, support, and counsel.

I am especially grateful to Susan Pearlman, who had the greatest influence on me and the conception of this book. Her unflagging enthusiasm for the French culture was overwhelmingly contagious and she remains responsible for instilling in me a love and fascination for the French language and its traditions.

I owe an enormous debt of gratitude to Dr. Ralph Baccash for all his hard work and significant contribution to this book. His insight into the *real* French language was indispensable. I feel extremely fortunate for having the opportunity to work with him and especially thankful for his wonderful friendship.

I consider myself so very lucky to have had the opportunity of working with PJ Dempsey, my editor at John Wiley & Sons. She made every step fun and exciting. Her constant inspiration, encouragement, and dedication to perfection was extraordinary. She has my deepest appreciation and lots of hugs!

Finally, I want to thank my family. The patience, love, and unrelenting support from my mother, Nancy, and from Tom was the driving force behind this book.

CONTENTS

INTRODUCTION

STREET FRENCH 1 has been updated with lots of new information to help you learn popular French slang. This entertaining guide, geared for the student who has had three or more years of French study, is a step-by-step approach to teaching the actual spoken language of France that is constantly used in movies, books, and day-to-day business, as well as among family and friends. Now you can learn quickly the secret world of slang as you are introduced to the "inside" language that even a ten-year veteran of formalized French would not understand!

STREET FRENCH 1 is designed to teach the essentials of colloquial French and slang in ten lessons. The material is organized to teach you first *how* to speak — i.e., how to use colloquial language, including the structure of a sentence, contractions, and shortcuts — then *what* to speak — i.e., slang.

This self-teaching guide is divided into six primary parts:

- **DIALOGUE**

  In this section, 20-30 slang words and expressions *(shown in boldface)* are presented in a French dialogue on the left-hand page. A translation of the dialogue appears on the opposite page. On the following page, the original French slang dialogue is presented again, this time using common contractions and reductions to give you an idea of how it may actually be heard in a conversation. This page is essential to anyone learning French since the natives rely heavily on contractions, reductions, and other shortcuts in pronunciation.

- **VOCABULARY**

  This section spotlights all of the slang terms that were used in the dialogue and offers:

  1. An example of usage for each entry.
  2. Another look at the example, this time written as it may *actually* be spoken by a native speaker. Here you will encounter two symbols:

     (1) ____ an underline indicating:

     a. where a contraction/reduction would be commonly made when spoken; or

b. where a personal pronoun has been added.
SEE: *Popular Usage of Objective Case Personal Pronouns & Ça, p. 102.*
(2) ~ a squiggle indicating where *ne* has been dropped.
SEE: *The Omission of "Ne," p. 14.*

3. An English translation of the example.
4. In addition, synonyms, antonyms, variations, or special notes are offered to give you a complete sense of the word or expression:

bourré(e) (être) *adj.* to be very drunk • (lit); to be stuffed (with alcohol).

example: Tu ne peux pas conduire comme ça. Tu es complètement **bourré**!

as pronounced: Tu ~ peux pas conduire comme ça. T'es complètement **bourré**!

translation: You can't drive like that. You're totally plastered!

NOTE: **bourrer** *v.* • (lit); to stuff, cram, pack tight.

■ PRACTICE THE VOCABULARY

These word games include all of the slang terms and idioms previously learned and will help you test yourself on your comprehension. Note that all exercises will be presented using contractions and reductions as learned in lesson one. *(The pages providing the answers to all the drills are indicated at the beginning of this section.)*

■ GRAMMAR SECTION

This section introduces unconventional "rules" regarding the usage of slang and colloquialisms in a clear, concise, and easy-to- understand style.

■ EXERCISES

Helpful drills are presented in this section to help test you on the previous GRAMMAR portion. The last GRAMMAR exercise of each chapter will include slang words and expressions from the preceding dialogue as a final review before continuing to the next chapter.

■ REVIEW

Following each sequence of five chapters is a summary review encompassing all the words and expressions learned up to that point.

The secret to learning **STREET FRENCH** is by following this simple checklist:

- Make sure that you have a good grasp on each section before proceeding to the drills. If you've made more than two errors in a particular drill, simply go back and review...then try again! *Remember:* This is a self-paced book, so take your time. You're not fighting the clock!
- It's very important that you feel comfortable with each chapter before proceeding to the next. Words learned along the way may crop up in the following dialogues. So feel comfortable before moving on!
- Make sure that you read the dialogues and drills aloud. This is an excellent way to become comfortable speaking colloquially and begin thinking like a native.

IMPORTANT: Slang must be used with discretion because it is an extremely casual "language" that certainly should not be practiced with formal dignitaries or employers that you are trying to impress! Most importantly, since a non-native speaker of French may tend to sound forced or artificial using slang, your first goal should be to *recognize and understand* these types of words. Once you feel that you have a firm grasp on the usage of the slang words and expressions presented in this book, try using some in your conversations for extra color!

Just as a student of formalized English would be rather shocked to run into words like *pooped, zonked,* and *wiped out,* and discover that they all go under the heading of "tired," you too will be surprised and amused to encounter a whole new array of terms and phrases usually hidden away in the French language and reserved only for the native speaker.

Welcome to the expressive and "colorful" world of slang!

Legend

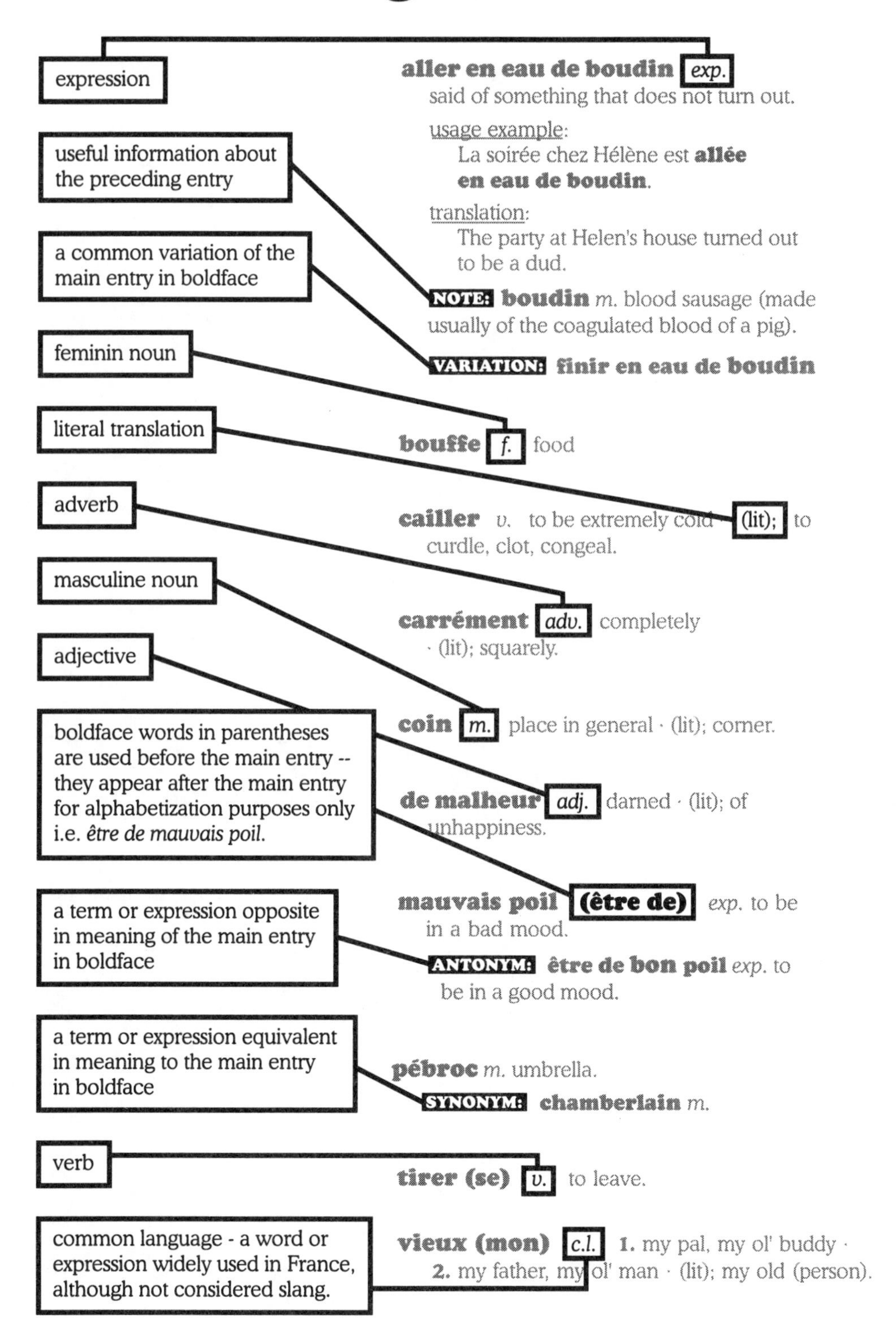
expression
useful information about the preceding entry
a common variation of the main entry in boldface
feminin noun
literal translation
adverb
masculine noun
adjective
boldface words in parentheses are used before the main entry -- they appear after the main entry for alphabetization purposes only i.e. être de mauvais poil.
a term or expression opposite in meaning of the main entry in boldface
a term or expression equivalent in meaning to the main entry in boldface
verb
common language - a word or expression widely used in France, although not considered slang.
aller en eau de boudin exp.
said of something that does not turn out.
usage example:
La soirée chez Hélène est allée en eau de boudin.
translation:
The party at Helen's house turned out to be a dud.
NOTE: boudin m. blood sausage (made usually of the coagulated blood of a pig).
VARIATION: finir en eau de boudin
bouffe f. food
cailler v. to be extremely cold (lit); to curdle, clot, congeal.
carrément adv. completely · (lit); squarely.
coin m. place in general · (lit); corner.
de malheur adj. darned · (lit); of unhappiness.
mauvais poil (être de) exp. to be in a bad mood.
ANTONYM: être de bon poil exp. to be in a good mood.
pébroc m. umbrella.
SYNONYM: chamberlain m.
tirer (se) v. to leave.
vieux (mon) c.l. 1. my pal, my ol' buddy · 2. my father, my ol' man · (lit); my old (person).

LEÇON UN

Il *Flotte* Encore!

*(It's **raining** again!)*

(A Typical Picnic)

Leçon Un

Dialogue in slang

Il Flotte Encore!

Alain: Tu sais, je viens de **claquer** tout mon **fric** sur la **bouffe**. Je dois être **carrément dingue**.

Carole: Quel **gueuleton** ça va être! Maintenant, on **se tire** pour trouver un **coin peinard** et **se taper la cloche**.

Alain: Tiens! C'est **génial**, ici! Regarde tous les **piafs**!

Carole: **Zut** alors! Il commence à **flotter** et je n'ai pas de **pébroc**.

Alain: **Je n'en reviens pas**, moi! Mais quelle **guigne**!

Carole: Quel **temps de chien**. Il **tombe des cordes**!

Alain: Oh, mais j'**en ai marre**. En été, on **crame** et en hiver on **caille**.

Carole: **Saucée de malheur**! Encore un pique-nique qui **est allé en eau de boudin**. (soupir)

Lesson One

Translation in English

Alain: Ya know, I just **blew** all my **money** on **food**. I must be **totally crazy**.

Carole: What a **feast** this is gonna be! Now **let's take off** to find a **quiet place** and **pig out**.

Alain: Hey! It's **terrific** here! Look at all the **birds**!

Carole: **Darn**! It's starting **to rain** and I don't have an **umbrella**.

Alain: **I don't believe this**! What **lousy luck**!

Carole: What **rotten weather**. It sure is **coming down**!

Alain: **I've really had it**! In the summer, **we fry** and in winter we **freeze**.

Carole: **Darn storm**! Another picnic **down the tubes**. (sigh)

Leçon Un

Dialogue in slang as it would be spoken

Y Flotte Encore!

Alain: Tu sais, j'viens d'**claquer** tout mon **fric** sur la **bouffe**. J'dois êt' **carrément dingue**.

Carole: Quel **gueuleton** ça va être! Maint'nant, on **s'tire** pour trouver un **coin peinard** et **s'taper la cloche**.

Alain: Tiens! C'est **génial**, ici! Regarde tous les **piafs**!

Carole: **Zut**, alors! Y commence à **flotter** et j'ai pas d'**pébroc**.

Alain: **J'en r'viens pas**, moi! Mais quelle **guigne**!

Carole: Quel **temps d'chien**. Y **tombe des cordes**!

Alain: Oh, mais j'**en ai marre**. En été, on **crame** et en hiver on **caille**.

Carole: **Saucée d'malheur**! Encore un pique-nique qui **est allé en eau d'boudin**. (soupir)

Vocabulary

aller en eau de boudin *exp.* to fizzle out (said of something that does not turn out).

example: Le projet **est allé en eau de boudin**.

as spoken: Le projet, l'**est allé en eau d'boudin**.

translation: The project **fizzled out**.

NOTE: **boudin** *m.* blood sausage.

VARIATION: **finir/partir en eau de boudin** *exp.*

bouffe *f.* food, "grub."

example: J'aime la **bouffe** française.

as spoken: [no change].

translation: I love French **food**.

NOTE: **bouffer** *v. (extremely popular)* to eat, "to chow down."

example: J'ai envie de **bouffer** quelque chose de chocolaté.

as spoken: J'ai envie d'**bouffer** quèque chose de chocolaté.

translation: I feel like **eating** something chocolaty.

cailler *v.* to be extremely cold • (lit); to curdle, clot, congeal.

example: Qu'est-ce qu'il fait froid! Je **caille**!

as spoken: Qu'est-c'qu'y fait froid! J'**caille**!

translation: It's so cold! I'm **freezing**!

ALSO: **se les cailler** *exp.* • (lit); to freeze them off. In this expression, "*les*" refers to "*les miches*" meaning "the loaves," also slang for "the buttocks."

example: Je **me les caille**!

as spoken: 1. Je **m'les caille**!

2. J'**me les caille**!

translation: I'm **freezing them** (my "buns") **off**!

carrément *adv.* completely • (lit); squarely.

example: Je ne peux pas le supporter. Il est **carrément** stupide.

as spoken: J'peux pas l'supporter. L'est **carrément** stupide.

translation: I can't stand him. He's **totally** stupid.

claquer *v.* to spend, to blow one's money.

example: Tu as **claqué** tout ton fric sur une robe?

as spoken: T'as **claqué** tout ton fric sur une robe?

translation: You **blew** all your money on a dress?

coin *m.* place in general.

example: Ce **coin**-là est tranquille.

as spoken: 1. C'**coin**-là, l'est tranquille.

2. L'est tranquille, c'**coin**-là.

translation: This **place** is very peaceful.

cramer *v.* to burn.

example (1): Je **crame** dans cette chaleur.

as spoken: J'**crame** dans c'te chaleur.

translation: I'm **burning up** in this heat.

example (2): J'ai **cramé** le dîner.

as spoken: J'ai **cramé** l'dîner.

translation: I **burned** the dinner.

de malheur *adj.* darned, that which causes unhappiness • (lit); of unhappiness.

example: Oh, cet ordinateur **de malheur** ne marche plus!

as spoken: Oh, c't'ordinateur **d'malheur** y ~ marche plus!

translation: Oh, this **darn** computer isn't working any more!

dingue (être) *adj.* to be crazy.

example: Tu penses que tu vas apprendre l'italien en deux semaines? Mais, tu es **dingue**, non?

as spoken: Tu penses que tu vas apprend' l'italien en deux s'maines? Mais, t'es **dingue**, non?

translation: You think you'll be able to learn Italian in two weeks? You're **crazy** or what?

VARIATION: **dingo (être)** *adj.*

SYNONYMS: *louftingue • cinglé(e) • marteau • barjo • siphonné(e), etc.*

flotter *v.* to rain • (lit); to float.

example: Il a **flotté** sans arrêt pendant nos vacances

as spoken: L'a **flotté** sans arrêt pendant nos vacances.

translation: It **rained** nonstop during our vacation.

NOTE: **flotte** *f.* • **1.** water • **2.** rain.

fric *m. (extremely popular)* money, "dough."

example: Je ne peux pas t'accompagner au cinéma ce soir. Je n'ai pas assez de **fric**.

as spoken: J'peux pas t'accompagner au ciné~ ce soir. J'ai pas assez d'**fric**.

translation: I can't go with you to the movies tonight. I don't have enough **money**.

SYNONYMS: *de l'oseille • du blé • des ronds • du pognon • des sous • du pèze, des picaillons • du grisbi • de la galette • du flouze*

génial(e) (être) *v. (extremely popular)* to be terrific, wonderful.

example: Regarde cette robe! Elle est **géniale**!

as spoken: Regarde c'te robe! L'est **géniale**!

translation: Look at this dress! It's **great**!

gueuleton *m.* a huge blow-out of a meal, a huge spread (of food).

example: On a fait un de ces **gueuletons** hier soir!

as spoken: On a fait un d'ces **gueuletons** hier soir!

translation: We had one heck of a **spread** last night!

NOTE (1): **gueule** *f.* mouth • (lit); mouth of an animal. When used in reference to a person, it becomes very derogatory and should be used with discretion.

NOTE (2): *un(e) de ces* is commonly used to mean "one heck of a..." For example: *Elle m'a raconté une de ces histoires!;* She told me one heck of a story!

ALSO: **"Ta gueule!"** *exp.* "Shut up!"

guigne *f.* bad luck.

example: J'ai la **guigne**.

as spoken: [no change].

translation: I have **bad luck**.

NOTE: **guignard(e)** *n.* unlucky individual.

SYNONYM: **poisse** *f.*

marre (en avoir) *exp.* to be fed up.

example: J'**en ai marre** de tous ces devoirs.

as spoken: J'**en ai marre** de tous ces d'voirs.

translation: I'm **fed up** with all this homework.

SYNONYM: **ras le bol (en avoir)** *exp.* (lit); to have had it up to the rim of the bowl.

pébroc *m.* umbrella.

example: N'oublie pas ton **pébroc**. Je pense qu'il va pleuvoir.

as spoken: ~ oublie pas ton **pébroc**. J'pense qu'y va pleuvoir.

translation: Don't forget your **umbrella**. I think it's going to rain.

SYNONYM (1): **chamberlain** *m.*

SYNONYM (2): **pépin** *m.*

piaf *m.* bird • (lit); Parisian sparrow.

example: Elle donne à manger aux **piafs**.

as spoken: È donne à manger aux **piafs**.

translation: She's feeding the **birds**.

revenir (ne pas en) *exp.* to disbelieve.

example: On a volé la voiture de Jean? Je **n'en reviens pas.**

as spoken: On a volé la voiture d'Jean? J'**en r'viens pas.**

translation: Jean's car was stolen? I **can't believe it**.

saucée *f.* • **1.** downpour • **2.** scolding, thrashing.

example (1): J'ai peur de conduire dans cette **saucée**.

as spoken: J'ai peur de conduire dans c'te **saucée**.

translation: I'm scared to drive in this **downpour**.

example (2): Elle lui a donné une vraie **saucée**.

as spoken: È lui a donné une vraie **saucée**.

translation: She gave him a real **thrashing**.

SYNONYM (1): **raclée** *f.* scolding, thrashing.

SYNONYM (2): **trempe** *f.* scolding, thrashing.

taper la cloche (se) *exp.* to eat well.

example: On **s'est bien tapé la cloche** chez tes vieux ce soir.

as spoken: [no change].

translation: We **ate up a storm** at your parents' house tonight.

NOTE: In the previous sentence, the term **vieux** was used, which is an extremely popular slang synonym for parents:
vieille *f.* mother • (lit); old woman.
vieux *m.* father • (lit); old man.
vieux (or **vioques**) *m.pl.* parents • (lit); "oldies."

temps de chien *exp.* bad weather • (lit); a dog's weather.

example: Il flotte depuis quatre jours! Quel **temps de chien**!

as spoken: Y flotte depuis quat' jours! Quel **temps d'chien**!

translation: It's been raining for four days! What **lousy weather**!

ALSO: **un froid de canard** *exp.* terribly cold weather • (lit); duck-hunting cold weather (when ducks migrate).

tirer (se) *v.* to leave.

example: Je dois **me tirer** tout de suite. Je suis en retard!

as spoken: J'dois **m'tirer** tout d'suite. J'suis en r'tard!

translation: I have **to leave** right away. I'm late!

SYNONYMS: *se tailler • se barrer • mettre les voiles • s'éclipser • prendre la tangente • mettre les bouts • débarrasser le plancher • plier bagages • se virer*

tomber des cordes *exp.* to rain heavily • (lit); to fall ropes (of rain).

example: Je comptais faire des courses aujourd'hui mais il **tombe des cordes** dehors.

as spoken: J'comptais faire des courses aujourd'hui mais y **tombe des cordes** dehors.

translation: I was planning on going shopping today but it's **pouring** outside.

Practice the Vocabulary 

(Answers to Lesson 1, p. 217)

A. Replace the word(s) in parentheses with the slang synonym from the right column.

1. Prends ton *(parapluie)* ____________ . Il commence à pleuvoir.
2. Qu'il fait chaud! Je *(brûle)* _________ !
3. Quel *(temps affreux)* ______________ !
4. J'ai *(dépensé)* ____________ tout mon fric au marché aux puces.
5. Regarde comme ça tombe. Mais, quelle *(averse)* ____________ !
6. Il *(pleut)* ___________ des cordes.
7. A Paris, les *(oiseaux)* _______________ volent partout.
8. Je suis en retard! Je dois *(partir)* _________________ tout de suite!
9. Tu habites dans un bon *(endroit)* ______ .
10. Ma mère a préparé un *(grand repas)* ____________ pour mon anniversaire.

A. coin
B. crame
C. pébroc
D. me tirer
E. gueuleton
F. saucée
G. claqué
H. temps de chien
I. tombe
J. piafs

B. Underline the appropriate word.

1. Tu as vu ce fou-là? Mais, il est (**doux**, **dingue**, **génial**)!
2. Il fait froid aujourd'hui. Je (**caille**, **colle**, **me cache**).
3. Je ne gagne jamais. J'ai la (**gueule**, **guigne**, **gorge**).
4. Quel bon restaurant! C'est sûr qu'on va se taper la (**crabe**, **clef**, **cloche**).
5. La (**bouffe**, **bague**, **barbe**) est délicieuse.
6. Je n'ai pas assez de (**fleurs**, **farine**, **fric**) pour acheter cette voiture.
7. Il est (**carrément**, **correctement**, **calmement**) bizarre, lui!
8. Ce projet est allé en eau de (**bidon**, **ballon**, **boudin**).

C. Match the French with the English translation.

☐ 1. It's starting to rain.	A. J'ai trop **bouffé** ce matin.
☐ 2. I ate too much this morning.	B. Je **n'en reviens pas**.
☐ 3. This car is fantastic!	C. Ces devoirs **de malheur**!
☐ 4. These darn assignments!	D. J'**en ai marre** d'y aller!
☐ 5. I can't believe it.	E. On a fait un **gueuleton** ce soir!
☐ 6. I'm relaxed today.	F. Il commence à **flotter**.
☐ 7. I'm freezing!	G. Cette voiture est **géniale**!
☐ 8. I'm fed up with going there!	H. Je suis **peinard** aujourd'hui.
☐ 9. We pigged out tonight.	I. Je **caille**!
☐ 10. I'm burning up!	J. Je **crame**!

A CLOSER LOOK I: *Contractions*

A. The omission of "e"

As in English, contractions are extremely important in conversational French. This is perhaps one of the most important aspects of understanding the spoken language and conversing like a native!

In certain cases, the letter "e" is commonly dropped from a word in order to make it easier to pronounce. This omission *only* takes place when the "e" (or *e caduc*, as it is called) is preceded and followed by one pronounced consonant. For example:

*sam**e**di* = ***sam'di***
*dev**e**nir* = ***dev'nir***
*J**e** te vois* = ***J'te vois***

However, it is important to note that in some cases the *e caduc* must not be omitted. If dropping the *e caduc* means that three consonants will appear one after the other, then you have just committed the ultimate phonetic *faux pas* by breaking the "*règle des trois consonnes*" (rule of three consonants). For example, if the *e caduc* were dropped in the word ***vendredri***, creating ***vendr'di***, it would be extremely difficult to pronounce and unpleasant to the French ear.

Below are some commonly heard contractions. Make sure to learn this section thoroughly before going on to the following chapters!

je = j'
Je veux aller en vancances.
J'veux aller en vacances.

ce = c'
Tu comprends ce qu'il dit?
Tu comprends c'qu'il dit?

me = m'
Tu me fais rire.
Tu m'fais rire.

de = d'
Elle a décidé de partir.
Elle a décidé d'partir.

te = t'
Tu vas te coucher maintenant?
Tu vas t'coucher maintenant?

le = l'
Elles vont le faire plus tard.
Elles vont l'faire plus tard.

se = s'
Jean se met en colère facilement.
Jean s'met en colère facilement.

que = qu'
Il faut que tu partes.
Il faut qu'tu partes.

NOTE (1): When *je* is followed by *me*, the contraction becomes either **j'me** or **je m'**: *J'me lève* • *Je m'lève*

NOTE (2): When **j'** *(je)* is followed by a word beginning with **c**, **f**, **p**, **q**, **s**, or **t**, it is commonly pronounced **sh**:

J'compte sur toi.
("Sh'compte")

J'quitte la maison
("Sh'quitte")

J'fais ça facilement.
("Sh'fais")

J'sais pas.
("Sh'sais" or "Shais")

J'peux pas y aller.
("Sh'peux")

J'te parle
("Sh'te")

NOTE (3): When **j'**, **c'**, **m'**, **d'**, **t'**, **l'**, or **s'** is followed by the same letter, the sound of that letter is simply held a little longer:

Elle a décidé de danser.
Elle a décidé d'danser.

Il va le lire.
Il va l'lire.

B. The omission of "ne"

In colloquial French, *ne* is omitted entirely:

Il **ne** va pas y aller. = *Il va pas y aller.*
Je **n'**ai pas d'argent sur moi. = *J'ai pas d'argent sur moi.*
Ne bouge pas = *Bouge pas!*
Je **ne** sais pas. = *J'sais pas.* (pronounced: *shè pas*)

C. The omission of "u" in "tu"

The letter **"u"** in **"tu"** may frequently be muted when followed by a vowel:

t**u** es = *t'es* **Ö** *(t'es pas)*
t**u** annonces = *t'annonces* **Ö** *(t'annonces pas)*
t**u** ouvres = *t'ouvres* **Ö** *(t'ouvres pas)*
t**u** invites = *t'invites* **Ö** *(t'invites pas)*

EXAMPLE: Tu avoues que tu es riche? = *T'avoues qu' t'es riche?*

D. The omission of "re"

In everyday speech, when something is difficult to pronounce, it may simply be slurred over or even dropped. These reductions, as they are called, are certainly common in spoken American-English. For example, going to = *gonna*, have to = *hafta*, what are you doing = *whatcha doin'*, did you eat yet = *djeetjet*, etc.

As seen so far in this section, the French commonly make reductions and contractions in their speech. The omission of "*re*" is also very common. For example: when the "*re*" ending is followed by a consonant, it is not easy to articulate quickly even for the native speaker of French. For this reason, the "*re*" sound is very often omitted entirely:

le pauv**re** chat = *le pauv'chat*
un, deux, trois, quat**re**, cinq = *un, deux, trois, quat', cinq*
not**re** maison = *not'maison*
vot**re** mère = *vot'mère*

The same applies to the "*re*" verbs:

EXAMPLE: Il va mett**re** son cahier sur la table.
Il va mett'son cahier sur la table.

Je vais prend**re** le train à onze heures pour êt**re** chez vous à midi.
J'vais prend' le train à onze heures pour êt'chez vous à midi.

Ça fait deux semaines que j'essaie de vend**re** ma vieille voiture!
Ça fait deux s'maines que j'essaie d'vend'ma vieille voiture!

NOTE: The **re** sound can only be dropped when it ends a word. Therefore, words like app**re**ndre, comp**re**ndre, cont**re**point, mont**re**r, etc., must retain the "*re*" sound.

Practice Using Contractions.

A. Rewrite the portion in parentheses using contractions.

Example:

Tu peux (me téléphoner) **m'téléphoner** *demain?*
(Je ne sais pas) **J'sais pas** *si (je peux)* **j'peux**.

1. *(Tu as)* ___________ faim?

2. *(Je te)* _____________ présente mon amie, Pascale.

3. *(Je comprends)* ________________________ bien
   (ce que) ___________ tu dis.

4. *(Je vais)* _____________ *(le voir)* _____________ plus tard.

5. *(Tu n'entends pas)* ____________________ le tonnerre dehors?

6. *(Je veux)* _____________ *(prendre)* _____________ mes vacances
   demain!

7. *(Je dois)* ________________ finir mes devoirs.

8. *(Je peux)* _____________ *(prendre)* _____________ le dernier métro
   si *(je me)* _____________ dépêche.

9. Qu'est-ce que *(je vais)* ___________ *(mettre)* ___________ ce soir?

10. *(Je pars)* _____________ tout *(de suite)* ___________ pour *(être)*
    ___________ chez toi à midi.

11. *(Je n'ai pas)* _______________ très faim.

12. *(Je ne peux pas)* _________________ *(le faire)* ___________ .

B. In the following paragraph, underline the letter(s) which would be dropped in every day conversation.

(Read the corrected paragraph aloud several times until you feel comfortable with the contractions.)

Example: *Je ne vais pas prendre votre voiture parce que les freins ne marchent pas bien.*

Aujourd'hui, je vais me lever de bonne heure pour passer la journée en ville. Je dois arriver vers midi pour déjeuner avec mes amis Irène et Jacques à notre café préféré. J'aime bien ce café parce que les prix ne sont pas astronomiques! Après, on va aller au parc prendre une glace! Si on a le temps, on va pousser jusqu'au jardin du Luxembourg.

A CLOSER LOOK II:

More Common Contractions

Contraction	Example	Note
celui = **c'ui**	Tu connais celui-là? *Tu connais* ***c'ui****-là?*	Contraction occurs only when *celui* is followed by **-ci** (pronounced *sui-si*) or **-là** (pronouned *sui-la*).
c'est un(e) = **c't'un(e)**	C'est un(e) bon(ne) ami(e). ***C't'un(e)*** *bon(ne) ami(e).*	
elle(s) = **è**	Elle m'énerve! **È** *m'énerve!* Elles sont belles. **È** *sont belles.*	This contraction is used only when followed by a consonant. Note that *elle* becomes **è** in the singular and plural.

Contraction	Example	Note
elle = **l'**	Elle est bizarre, elle. ***L'****est bizarre, elle.*	Since this is also the same contraction for *il*, it should *only* be used when it's obvious that the subject is feminine. In the example, *elle* was added to the end of the sentence for clarity.
elles = **è'z'**	Elles écoutent la radio. ***È'z'****écoutent la radio.*	This contraction is used only when followed by a vowel. Note that in the pural, **l'** is replaced by **è'z**.
il faut = **faut**	Il faut que je parte. 1. ***Faut*** *qu'je parte.* 2. ***Faut*** *que j'parte.*	**il** may be dropped in all tenses: **faudrait** (que), **fallait** (que), etc.
il y a = **y a**	Il y a du monde ici! ***Y a*** *du monde ici!*	Also, **y aurait**, **y avait**, **y a eu**, etc. *Note:* When used as an abbreviation of **il y a**, **y a** is articulated as one syllable: **ya**.
il = **y** (when followed by a consonant)	Il va venir m'aider. ***Y*** *va v'nir m'aider.*	This contraction only occurs when followed by a consonant.
il = **l'** (when followed by a vowel)	Il est bizarre, lui! ***L'****est bizarre, lui!*	Since this is also the same contraction as for *elle*, it should *only* be used when it's obvious that the subject is masculine. In the example, *lui* was added at the end of the sentence for clarity.

Contraction	Example	Note
ils = **y**	Ils vont au magasin. ***Y*** *vont au magasin.*	This contraction is used only when followed by a consonant.
ils = **y z' (or z')**	Ils ont de la chance. 1. ***Y z'****ont d'la chance.* 2. ***Z'****ont d'la chance.*	This contraction is used only when followed by a vowel.
parce que = **pasque** (and **parc'que**)	Il sourit parce qu'il est content. *Il sourit* ***pasqu'****il est content.*	
petit(e) = **p'tit(e)**	Il est petit. *Il est* ***p'tit****.* Elle est petite. *Elle est* ***p'tite****.*	
peut-être = **p't'êt'**	Peut-être qu'il est malade. ***P't'êt'****qu'il est malade.*	
quelque = **quèque**	Tu veux quelque chose à boire? *Tu veux quèque chose à boire?*	This contraction is commonly used with *quelque chose (kèk chose)* and *quelque part (kèk part)*.
qui = **qu'**	Aujourd'hui, j'ai rencontré une dame qui a cent ans! *Aujourd'hui, j'ai rencontré une dame* ***qu'****a cent ans!*	Thie contraction occurs when *qui* is followed by a verb beginning with a vowel. **Note:** Contraction does not occur when *qui* begins a sentence.
s'il te plaît = **s'te plaît**	Passe-moi le beurre, s'il te plaît. *Passe-moi l'beurre, s'te plaît.*	

Exercises

A. Write in the appropriate contraction.

1. ______________________ c'est un

2. ______________________ il y a

3. ______________________ celui-là

4. ______________________ il faut

5. ______________________ il est

6. ______________________ quelque chose

7. ______________________ il parle

8. ______________________ qui est

9. ______________________ il y avait

10. ______________________ elle rit

B. Fill in the blanks with the common pronunciation of the word(s) in boldface.

(There is one slang word in each sentence below from the dialogue. Can you recognize it?)

1. **Il a** ________ commencé à pleuvoir. **Je dois** ________________ **prendre** ____________ mon pébroc.

2. **Il** ________ va très bien **parce** ____________ qu'**il** ____________ va **se tirer** ____________________ pour les vacances.

3. **C'est un** ____________ film génial.

4. **Il y a** ____________ beaucoup **de** ____________ piafs dehors.

5. Tu peux **me** __________ prêter du fric **s'il te plaît** ____________ ?

6. **Ils ont** ____________ fait un gueuleton ce soir.

7. **Je crois** ____________ qu'**elle** __________ veut **me** ____________ parler **de** ____________ son accident d'auto. C'est la deuxième fois **que** ________ ça lui arrive ce mois-ci! Quelle guigne!

8. **Je n'ai** ____________ pas **de** __________ fric.

9. J'en ai marre! **Je ne sais** ____________ pas **ce qu'il** ____________ **me** ____________ dit!

10. **Ils** ____________ vont pas à la plage **parce qu'il** ____________ tombe des cordes.

DICTATION

Test Your Aural Comprehension.

(This dictation can be found in Appendix A on page 234)

If you are following along with your cassette, you will now hear a paragraph containing many of the terms from this section. The paragraph will be read at normal conversational speed (which may actually seem fast to you at first). In addition, the words will be pronounced as you would actually hear them in a conversation, including many common reductions.

The first time the paragraph is presented, simply listen in order to get accustomed to the speed and heavy use of reductions. The paragraph will then be read again with a pause after each group of words to give you time to write down what you heard. The third time the paragraph is read, follow along with what you have written.

LEÇON DEUX

Quel *Boui-Boui!*

*(What a **dive**!)*

(Au Restaurant)

Leçon Deux

Dialogue in slang

Quel Boui-Boui!

Régis: J'espère que ce n'est pas un **boui-boui** comme celui d'hier soir. Il était **cradingue** celui-là!

Nélie: Ne t'inquiète pas. Ce **resto** est **de première**. Regarde comme c'est **nickel**!

Régis: Oui, c'est vrai. Mais, je commence à avoir les **crocs**, moi. Je vais **me goinfrer** ce soir.

Nélie: Moi aussi! Je m'**en pourlèche les badigoinces** d'avance.

Régis: Tu as vu ces prix? Deux cents **balles** pour du **brouille-ménage**? La **boustifaille** à ce resto, ça doit être le **coup de fusil**!

Nélie: Calme-toi! C'est moi qui **régale**. Tu prends l'**apéro**, toi? **Voilà** le **barman**.

Régis: Ce **guindal** de flotte me suffit. Quand je **picole**, je deviens **bourré** en un **rien de temps...** un vrai **poivrot**!

Nélie: Mais le serveur pourrait toujours te **filer** du café si tu préfères. Qu'est-ce qu'il est devenu au fait, notre serveur?

Régis: Génial! Pas de **douloureuse**!

Nélie: Et s'il ne **se pointe** pas dans deux **z'gondes**, pas de **pourliche**!

Leçon Deux

Translation in English

Régis: I hope this isn't a **dive** like the one last night. It was **filthy**!

Nélie: Don't worry. This **restaurant** is **the best**. Look how **spotless** it is!

Régis: Yeah, that's true. I'm getting kind of **hungry**. I'm gonna **pork out** tonight.

Nélie: Me, too! **My mouth is already watering**.

Régis: Did you see these prices? Two hundred **francs** for **ordinary red wine**? The **food** at this restaurant must be **expensive**!

Nélie: Relax! I'm **paying**. You want a **cocktail**? **There's** the **barman**.

Régis: This **glass** of water is just fine. When I **drink**, I get **bombed in no time flat**... a real **drunk**!

Nélie: But the waiter could always **give** you some coffee, if you prefer. What happened to our waiter anyway?

Régis: Great! No **check**!

Nélie: And if he doesn't **show up** in two **seconds**, no **tip**!

Leçon Deux

Dialogue in slang as it would be spoken

Quel Boui-Boui!

Régis: J'espère qu'c'est pas un **boui-boui** comme celui d'hier soir. L'était **cradingue** c'ui-là!

Nélie: T'inquiète pas. C'**resto**, l'est **d'première**. Regarde comme c'est **nickel**!

Régis: Oui, c'est vrai. Mais j'commence à avoir les **crocs**, moi. J'vais **m'goinfrer** ce soir.

Nélie: Moi aussi! J'm'**en pourlèche les badigoinces** d'avance.

Régis: T'as vu ces prix? Deux cents **balles** pour du **brouille-ménage**? La **boustifaille** à c'resto, ça doit êt' le **coup d'fusil**!

Nélie: Calme-toi! C'est moi qui **régale**. Tu prends l'**apéro**, toi? **V'là** l'**barman**.

Régis: C'**guindal** de flotte, ça m'suffit. Quand j'**picole**, j'deviens **bourré** en un **rien de temps...** un vrai **poivrot**!

Nélie: Mais l'serveur, y pourrait toujours te **filer** du café si tu préfères. Qu'est-c'qu'y est dev'nu au fait, not'serveur?

Régis: Génial! Pas d'**douloureuse**!

Nélie: Et s'y **s'pointe** pas dans deux **z'gondes**, pas d'**pourliche**!

Vocabulary

apéro *m.* cocktail, apéritif.

example: Je prends toujours l'**apéro** avant le dîner.

as spoken: J'prends toujours l'**apéro** avant l'dîner.

translation: I always have a **cocktail** before dinner.

balle *f. (extremely popular)* one franc • (lit); ball or bullet.

example: J'ai oublié mon portefeuille chez moi. Tu peux me passer cent **balles**?

as spoken: J'ai oublié mon portefeuille chez moi. Tu peux m'passer cent **balles**?

translation: I forgot my wallet at home. Can you lend me a hundred **francs**?

NOTE (1): Of all the slang synonyms for money, this is one of the most popular.

NOTE (2): As shown above, the literal translation of *balle* is "ball." It's interesting to note that the French have two words for "ball" depending on its size. The feminine noun *balle* is used for smaller balls, and the masculine noun *ballon* is used for larger ones. For example: *une **balle** de ping-pong, tennis, golf, baseball* • *un **ballon** de football, basketball, volleyball.*

barman *m.* bartender (borrowed from English).

example: Mon frère est **barman** et bosse toujours la nuit. Il rentre à 4h tous les matins!

as spoken: Mon frère, l'est **barman** et bosse toujours la nuit. Y rentre à 4h tous les matins!

translation: My brother's a **bartender** and always works at night. He comes home at 4:00 every morning!

ANTONYM: **bargirl** *n.* woman bartender.

NOTE: **bosser** is a very popular slang verb meaning "to work."

boui-boui *m.* bad restaurant, a dive or "greasy spoon."

example: Comment tu arrives à bouffer dans ce **boui-boui**?

as spoken: Comment t'arrives à bouffer dans c'**boui-boui**?

translation: How do you manage eating in this **dive**?

bourré(e) (être) *adj.* to be very drunk • (lit); to be stuffed (with alcohol).

example: Tu ne peux pas conduire comme ça. Tu es complètement **bourré**!

as spoken: Tu ~ peux pas conduire comme ça. T'es complètement **bourré**!

translation: You can't drive like that. You're totally **plastered**!

NOTE: **bourrer** *v.* • (lit); to stuff, cram, pack tight.

boustifaille *f.* food, "grub."

example: Hier soir, ma tante nous a préparé de la **boustifaille** que je n'ai pas pu manger! C'était dégueulasse!

as spoken: Hier soir, ma tante è nous a préparé d'la **boustifaille** qu' j'ai pas pu manger! C'était dégueulasse!

translation: Last night, my aunt made **food** for us that I couldn't eat! It was gross!

SYNONYM: **mangeaille** *f.* (from the verb *manger* meaning "to eat").

NOTE: (1) **boustifailler** *v.* to eat, "to chow down."

NOTE: (2) The adjective **dégueulasse**, meaning "disgusting" or "gross," is one of the most widely used words in the French repertoire. It may also be abbreviated to **dégueu**.

ALSO: **dégueuler** *v.* to throw up, to barf.

brouille-ménage *m.* humorous for ordinary red wine.

example: Tu veux du **brouille-ménage** avec ton repas?

as spoken: [no change]

translation: Would you like some **red wine** with your meal?

NOTE: **brouiller** *v.* to mix up, stir up • **ménage** *m.* household. This literally translates as "something that stirs up the household" since husbands and wives would get into fights after having too much to drink.

coup de fusil (être le) *exp.* to be exorbitantly expensive • (lit); be a gunshot.

example: Tu as claqué mille balles au restaurant?! C'est **le coup de fusil**!

as spoken: T'as claqué mille balles au resto?! C'est **l'coup d'fusil**!

translation: You blew a thousand francs at the restaurant?! That's **outrageously expensive**!

cradingue *adj.* filthy.

example: La maison de Robert est toujours **cradingue**!

as spoken: La maison d'Robert, l'est toujours **cradingue**!

translation: Robert's house is always **filthy**!

VARIATION (1): **cracra** *adj. (extremely popular).*

VARIATION (2): **crado** *adj.*

VARIATION (3): **craspèque** *adj.*

crocs (avoir les) *m.pl.* to be very hungry • (lit); to have fangs.

example: Tu **as les crocs**? Ce n'est pas possible! Tu viens de bouffer!

as spoken: T'**as les crocs**? C'est pas possible! Tu viens d'bouffer!

translation: You're **hungry**? That's impossible! You just ate!

NOTE (1): The "cs" in **crocs** is silent.

NOTE (2): **crocs** *m.pl.* slang for "teeth" • (lit); fangs.

douloureuse *f.* bill (in a restaurant) • (lit); that which causes pain.

example: Ah! Voilà la **douloureuse**!

as spoken: Ah! V'là la **douloureuse**!

translation: Ah! There's the **bill**!

NOTE: Derived from the feminine noun "*douleur*" meaning "pain."

filer *v.* to give, hand over.

example: **File**-moi ça tout de suite!

as spoken: **File**-moi ça tout d'suite!

translation: **Hand** that **over** right now!

goinfrer (se) *v.* to eat a lot, to "pork out."

example: J'ai les crocs. Je vais **me goinfrer** ce soir.

as spoken: J'ai les crocs. J'vais **m'goinfrer** c'soir.

translation: I'm very hungry. I'm going **to pig out** tonight.

NOTE: **goinfre** *m.* one who makes a pig of oneself, an "oinker."

SYNONYM: **s'empiffrer** *v.*

guindal *m.* glass (of water, etc.).

example: Tu veux un **guindal** de flotte?

as spoken: [no change]

translation: Do you want a **glass** of water?

nickel *adj.* very clean, "spotless."

example: Ta maison est toujours aussi **nickel**?

as spoken: Ta maison, l'est toujours aussi **nickel**?

translation: Your house is always this **spotless**?

picoler *v.* to drink alcohol.

example: Je viens d'apprendre que le patron **picole** chaque matin avant d'arriver au boulot.

as spoken: J'viens d'apprend' que l'patron, y **picole** chaque matin avant d'arriver au boulot.

translation: I just learned that the boss **drinks** every morning before coming to work.

NOTE (1): **pictance** *f.* alcohol.

NOTE (3): **boulot** *m.* *(extremely popular)* work, the "grind."

pointer (se) *v.* to arrive, to show up.

example: Si Anne ne **se pointe** pas dans deux minutes, je me tire!

as spoken: Si Anne, è ~ **s'pointe** pas dans deux minutes, j'me tire!

translation: If Anne doesn't **show up** in two minutes, I'm leaving!

NOTE (1): **pointer** *v.* • (lit); to sprout up.

NOTE (2): **tirer (se)** *v.* to leave • (lit); to pull oneself (away).

poivrot *m.* drunkard.

example: Il t'apprend à conduire? Mais c'est un **poivrot**! Tu n'as pas remarqué?

as spoken: Y t'apprend à conduire? Mais c't'un **poivrot**! T'as pas r'marqué?

translation: He's teaching you how to drive? But he's a **drunk**! You didn't notice?

SYNONYM: **soûlard** (also spelled: *saoûlard*).

pourlécher les badigoinces (s'en) *exp.* to lick one's lips over something • (lit); to lick one's chops over something.

example: Demain, ma mère va préparer du coq au vin. Je **m'en pourlèche les badigoinces** d'avance!

as spoken: Demain, ma mère, è va préparer du coq au vin. J'**m'en pourlèche les badigoinces** d'avance!

translation: Tomorrow, my mother is going to make chicken in red wine. **My mouth is** already **watering**!

première (de) *adj.* excellent, first-rate.

example: Cette soirée est **de première**!

as spoken: Cette soirée, l'est **d'première**!

translation: This party's **top drawer**!

NOTE: This is a common shortened version of **de première classe** meaning "of first class quality."

régaler *v.* to treat • (lit); to entertain, to regale.

example: C'est moi qui **régale**!

as spoken: [no change]

translation: It's **on me**!

resto *m.* abbreviation of "restaurant."

example: Ce **resto** coûte trop cher.

as spoken: C'**resto**, y coûte trop cher.

translation: This **restaurant** is too expensive.

NOTE: This abbreviation got its name from Coluche, the late, popular comedian who launched a chain of low-priced eateries for the destitute. These restaurants were called *"les restos du cœur."*

v'là *interj.* a commonly heard reduction of "*voilà.*"

example: **V'là** le patron! Tire-toi!

as spoken: **V'là** l'patron! Tire-toi!

translation: **There's** the boss! Scram!

NOTE: The verb **se tirer** (meaning "to scram") is extremely popular in French slang. In fact, the Woody Allen classic *Take the Money and Run* is translated in French as *Prends l'Oseille et Tire-Toi*. The term *oseille* is commonly used in French slang to mean "money"; its literal translation is "sorrel," which is a green, leafy vegetable.

z'gonde *f.* a commonly heard reduction of "seconde."

example: Attends deux **z'gondes**. J'arrive.

as spoken: [no change]

translation: Wait two **seconds**. I'll be right there.

Practice The Vocabulary

(Answers to Lesson 2, p. 218)

A. Underline the definition.

1. **boustifaille:** a. boisson b. nourriture
2. **guindal:** a. verre b. restaurant
3. **avoir les crocs**: a. avoir de l'argent b. avoir faim
4. **nickel**: a. sale b. propre
5. **cradingue:** a. sale b. beau
6. **balle:** a. franc b. voiture
7. **filer:** a. montrer b. donner
8. **poivrot:** a. garçon b. alcoolique
9. **picoler:** a. courir b. boire
10. **se pointer:** a. arriver b. partir

B. CROSSWORD

Fill in the crossword puzzle on the opposite page by choosing from the list below.

APERO
BALLE
BOUI
BOUSTIFAILLE
BROUILLE
CRADINGUE
CROCS
FILER
FUSIL
GOINFRER
GUINDAL
NICKEL
PICOLER
POINTER
POIVROT
RÉGALER

ACROSS

9. ______ *m.* drunkard.
16. ______**-ménage** *m.* humorous for red wine.
20. ______ *m.* glass (of water, etc.).
27. ______ **(se)** *v.* to eat a lot, to "pork out."
30. ______ *adj.* filthy.
32. ______ *f. (extremely popular)* one franc.
37. ______ *v.* to treat • (lit); to entertain, to regale.
46. **coup de** ______ **(être le)** *exp.* to be exorbitantly expensive • (lit); be a gunshot.
50. ______ *adj.* very clean, "spotless."
53. ______ **(se)** *v.* to arrive, to show up.

DOWN

7. **boui-**______ *m.* bad restaurant, a dive or "greasy spoon."
10. ______ *m.* cocktail, apéritif.
16. ______ *f.* food, "grub."
35. ______ **(avoir les)** *m.pl.* to be very hungry.
36. ______ *v.* to drink alcohol.
46. ______ *v.* to give, hand over.

CROSSWORD PUZZLE

7
9 10
16
20
27
30
32
35 36
37
46
50
53

C. Complete the sentence by choosing the appropriate words from the list. Give the correct form of the verb.

badigoinces	**brouille-ménage**	**nickel**
balles	**cradingues**	**poivrot**
boui-boui	**douloureuse**	**régaler**
bourrée	**fusil**	**se goinfrer**

1. Quel repas fabuleux! J'm'en pourlèche les ____________ d'avance!
2. Regarde cette fille! J'crois qu'elle a trop bu. L'est complèment ____________ !
3. T'as vu la ____________ ? L'est cher, c'café!
4. Tes vêtements, y sont ____________ ! Va les laver tout d'suite!
5. T'inquiète pas du prix. C'est moi qui ____________ .
6. Mon cousin, y boit tout l'temps. C't'un vrai ____________ .
7. J'veux picoler, moi. Où est l'____________ ?
8. T'as vu le prix des desserts? Quel coup d' ____________ !
9. Tu veux manger ici? Mais c't'un ____________ !
10. J'ai très faim! J'ai envie de ____________ ce soir.
11. Devine combien j'ai dépensé pour cette chemise... mille ____________ !
12. Ta maison, l'est toujours ____________ ! C'est jamais cradingue chez toi.

A CLOSER LOOK:
The Structure of a Question

A. Inversion and "est-ce que" forms

The structure of a question is extremely important when trying to speak like a native. Even in English, there is a "relaxed" way of speaking. Questions are often in the form of statements:

Example:
You're going to Europe next week?

This construction is even more important when using slang. If one were to use slang terms in a sentence that was constructed and articulated academically, it would sound unnatural:

Example:
Do you think she is going to be so ticked off at him that she will freak out in front of the whole class?

More informal pronunciation actually sounds less jarring:

Example:
Ya think she's gonna be so ticked off ad'em she's gonna freak oud' in fronna the whole class?

In colloquial French, a question is almost always constructed this way, as a statement with a question mark at the end. Traditionally, the **inversion** and **est-ce que** forms are used in questions:

Inversion form:
Veux-tu déjeuner chez moi?

"est-ce que" form:
Est-ce que tu veux déjeuner chez moi?

However, in colloquial French, these two forms are rarely used:

Veux-tu déjeuner chez moi? =
Tu veux déjeuner chez moi?

Est-ce que tu vas mieux? =
Tu vas mieux?

IMPORTANT: Because slang is a casual and informal "language," the structure of any sentence containing slang should be casual and informal as well or it may tend to sound phony!

B. The structure of a question when using interrogative terms

The previous rule also applies to interrogative terms: **combien (de)**, **comment**, **où**, **pourquoi**, **quand**, **quel(le)**, **qui** and **quoi**. The interrogative term is placed at the beginning of the statement, transforming it into a question.

Interrogative Terms	Examples
combien (how much)	Combien pèses-tu? = *Combien tu pèses?* (How much do you weigh?)
combien de (how many, how much)	Combien d'enfants a-t-elle? = *Combien elle en a, d'enfants?* (How many children does she have?) *Note:* This is a strange one! In academic French, we are taught that **de** always follows **combien** when meaning "how many." However, in colloquial French, the object is placed at the end of the question as well as between the subject and verb in the form of the redundant pronoun **en**.
comment (how)	Comment vas-tu? = *Comment tu vas?* (How are you?)
où (where)	Où vas-tu maintenant? = *Où tu vas maintenant?* (Where are you going now?) *Note:* This also applies to **d'où**: D'où viens-tu? = *D'où tu viens?* (Where do you come from?)

Interrogative Terms	Examples
pourquoi (why)	Pourquoi as-tu acheté ça? = *Pourquoi t'as acheté ça?* (Why did you buy that?)
quand (when)	Quand est-ce qu'ils vont arriver? = *Quand ils vont arriver?* (When are they going to arrive?)
quel(le) (what/which)	Quelle heure est-il? = *Quelle heure il est?* (What time is it?)
qui (who and whom - as objects)	Qui rencontres-tu à l'aéroport? = *Qui tu rencontres à l'aéroport?* (Who are you meeting at the airport?) *Note:* This also applies to **à qui**, **avec qui**, **pour qui**, etc. For example: *A qui tu parles?* *Avec qui tu danses?* *Pour qui t'as fait ça?*
quoi (what)	Qu'est-ce que tu vas porter ce soir? = *Tu vas porter quoi ce soir?* *Note:* **quoi** is a little different from the other interrogative pronouns because it never begins a statement but rather follows the verb. *Also: c'est quoi, ça?* is an extremely common colloquial substitute for "qu'est-ce que c'est?"
à quoi (to what)	À quoi penses-tu? = *À quoi tu penses?* (What are you thinking about?)
de quoi (about what)	De quoi parles-tu? = *De quoi tu parles?* (What are you talking about?)

Practice Asking a Question

A. Rewrite the question in colloquial French using contractions where appropriate.

Examples:

Pourquoi as-tu fait ça?	Qu'est-ce qu'y veut, lui?
Pourquoi t'as fait ça?	***Y veut quoi, lui?***

1. Qui vas-tu aider?

   ____?

2. Quand veux-tu partir?

   ____?

3. Quelle heure est-il?

   ____?

4. Pourquoi n'aimes-tu pas ça?

   ____?

5. Comment va-t-il aller à la plage?

   ____?

6. Qu'est-ce que tu écris?

   ____?

7. D'où vient-il?

   ____?

8. Combien de pantalons as-tu?

   ____?

9. Désires-tu m'accompagner?

    ______________________________________?

10. Prends-tu l'autobus?

    ______________________________________?

11. Sais-tu conduire?

    ______________________________________?

12. Aimes-tu ça?

    ______________________________________?

B. Write the question that goes with the answer.

Examples:

Y va aller au resto avec Nicholas.

(avec qui) ***Avec qui y va aller au resto?***

J'vais prend' la boustifaille.

(quoi) ***Tu vas prend' quoi?***

1. J'vais parler du boui-boui à ma mère.

    (à qui) ______________________________?

2. È regarde le poivrot.

    (qui) ______________________________?

3. J'veux un apéro.

    (quoi) ______________________________?

4. J'vais commander c'brouille-ménage.

    (quoi) ______________________________?

5. J'vais parler au barman.
   (à qui) ____ ?

6. J'ai hérité d'un million d'balles.
   (quoi) ____ ?

7. Elle a trois enfants.
   (combien) ____ ?

8. Y va s'goinfrer à la Tour d'Argent.
   (où) ____ ?

9. È va picoler avec Robert.
   (avec qui) ____ ?

10. Y va laver c'guindal.
    (quoi) ____ ?

DICTATION

Test Your Aural Comprehension.

(This dictation can be found in Appendix A on page 235)

If you are following along with your cassette, you will now hear a paragraph containing many of the terms from this section. The paragraph will be read at normal conversational speed (which may actually seem fast to you at first). In addition, the words will be pronounced as you would actually hear them in a conversation, including many common reductions.

The first time the paragraph is presented, simply listen in order to get accustomed to the speed and heavy use of reductions. The paragraph will then be read again with a pause after each group of words to give you time to write down what you heard. The third time the paragraph is read, follow along with what you have written.

LEÇON TROIS

On a *Piqué* Ma *Téloche!*

(Someone ***swiped*** *my* ***television****!)*

(Une Nuit Mouvementée)

Leçon Trois

Dialogue in slang

On a Piqué Ma Téloche!

Jean: **Salut**, Marc. Mais, tu as l'air **lessivé**!

Marc: **Tu parles**! Hier soir, j'étais dans mon **plumard**, quand j'ai entendu un **mec** qui **se baladait** à l'extérieur de la **baraque** à côté de chez moi.

Jean: C'était un **casseur**?

Marc: **Exact**. Comme il ne pouvait pas **encarrer** par la **lourde**, il a **bousillé** la fenêtre. Quel **bordel**!

Jean: **Probable** qu'il voulait **barboter** une **téloche** ou quelque chose de ce genre.

Marc: C'est sûr... pour la **mettre au clou**. Alors, j'ai appelé la **flicaille**, bien sûr.

Jean: Elle a **radiné** tout de suite?

Marc: Oui, mais le mec **s'est carapaté**. Je suppose qu'il s'est **planqué** quelque part.

Jean: Probable! S'il se **fait agrafer**, on va le **fourrer** au **placard**. C'est sûr qu'il va **écoper** quelques **piges**.

Marc: Alors, après qu'on m'a **cuisiné** pendant toute une heure, je n'ai pas pu me rendormir.

Jean: Quelle **histoire**!

Leçon Trois

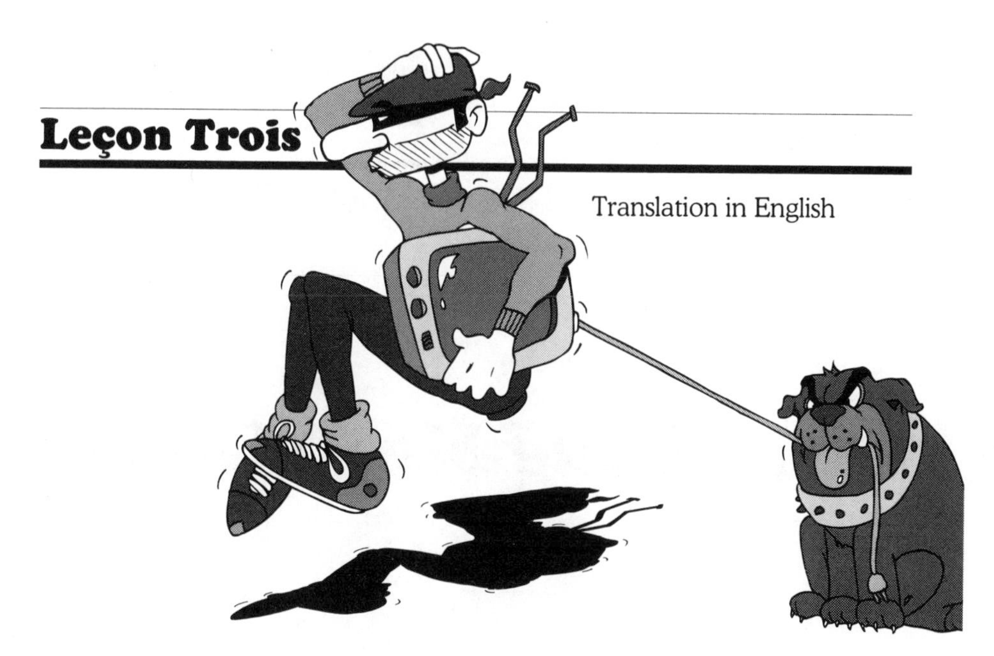

Translation in English

Jean: **Hi**, Marc. You look **wiped out**!

Marc: **You said it**! Last night, I was in my **bed** when I heard a **guy** who was **walking around** outside the **house** next to mine.

Jean: Was it a **burglar**?

Marc: Exactly. Since he couldn't **get in** through the **door**, he **busted** the window. What a **mess**!

Jean: He **probably** wanted to **rip off** a **television** or something like that.

Marc: Sure... in order to **hock it**. So, I called the **cops**, of course.

Jean: Did they **show up** right away?

Marc: Yeah, but the guy **darted away**. I suppose he **hid** somewhere.

Jean: Probably! If he **gets himself caught**, they'll **throw him** in the **slammer**. He's sure to get **slapped with** a couple of **years**.

Marc: So, after getting the **third degree** for an entire hour, I couldn't get back to sleep

Jean: What an **adventure**!

Leçon Trois

Dialogue in slang as it would be spoken

On a Piqué Ma Téloche!

Jean: **Salut**, Marc. Mais, t'as l'air **lessivé**!

Marc: **Tu parles**! Hier soir, j'étais dans mon **plumard** quand j'ai entendu un **mec** qui **s'baladait** à l'extérieur d'la **baraque** à côté d'chez moi.

Jean: C'était un **casseur**?

Marc: **Exact**. Comme y pouvait pas **encarrer** par la **lourde**, l'a **bousillé** la fenêtre. Quel **bordel**!

Jean: **Probable** qu'y voulait **barboter** une **téloche** ou quèque chose de c'genre.

Marc: C'est sûr… pour la **mettre au clou**. Alors, j'ai appelé la **flicaille**, bien sûr.

Jean: Y z'ont **radiné** tout d'suite?

Marc: Oui, mais l'mec y **s'est carapaté**. J'suppose qu'y s'est **planqué** quèque part.

Jean: Probable! S'y **s'fait agrafer**, on va l'**fourrer** au **placard**. C'est sûr qu'y va **écoper** quèques **piges**.

Marc: Alors, après qu'on m'a **cuisiné** pendant toute une heure, j'ai pas pu m'rendormir.

Jean: Quelle **histoire**!

Vocabulary

agrafer (se faire) *v.* to get arrested • (lit); to fasten by means of a hook, clasp, or clip; to staple.

example: Le voleur a essayé de s'enfuir, mais il **s'est fait agrafer**.

as spoken: Le voleur, l'a essayé d's'enfuir, mais y **s'est fait agrafer**.

translation: The thief tried to get away, but he got **nabbed**.

NOTE: **agrafer** *v.* to arrest.

balader (se) *v.* to stroll.

example: J'aime bien **me balader** le long de la Seine pour regarder le coucher de soleil.

as spoken: J'aime bien **m'balader** l'long d'la Seine pour regarder l'coucher d'soleil.

translation: I like **to stroll** along the Seine to watch the sunset.

NOTE (1): **balade** *f.* stroll.

example: Tu veux faire une **balade** avec moi?

as spoken: [no change]

translation: Do you want to take a **stroll** with me?

NOTE (2): **baladeur** *m.* Walkman.

baraque *f.* house *(extremely popular)* • (lit); hut.

example: Michelle habite dans une grande **baraque**.

as spoken: Michelle, l'habite dans une grande **baraque**.

translation: Michelle lives in a big **house**.

bordel *m.* an unruly mess or confusion • (lit); bordello.

example: Arrête de foutre le **bordel** dans ta chambre! Tu vas la ranger tout de suite!

as spoken: Arrête de fout' le **bordel** dans ta chambre! Tu vas la ranger tout d'suite!

translation: Stop making such a **mess** in your room! You're going to clean it up right now!

NOTE (1): **foutre le bordel** *exp.* to make a mess • (lit); to turn into a bordello (*foutre* is a popular slang verb meaning "to put").

NOTE (2): The verb **foutre** is *extremely* popular in French and is used in zillions of expressions in all levels of society. Although it originally had a sexual connotation in the 17th century, today it simply means **1.** to put, "to throw" • **2.** to give • to do.

example (1): J'ai **foutu** mes affaires dans l'armoire.

as spoken: [no change]

translation: I **threw** my things in the closet.

example (2): Le prof m'a **foutu** une sale note à l'examen.

as spoken: Le prof, y m'a **foutu** une sale note à l'examen.

translation: The teacher **gave** me a lousy grade on the test.

example (3): Il ne **fout** rien toute la journée.

as spoken: Y ~ **fout** rien toute la journée.

translation: He doesn't **do** a thing all day.

NOTE (3): Some other common expressions using **foutre** are:
C'est foutu! = It's ruined!
Fous-moi la paix! = Leave me alone!
Fous le camp! = Beat it!
Je m'en fous! = I don't care!
Rien à foutre! = Nothing doing!
se foutre de quelqu'un = to make fun of someone

bousiller *v.* to break or damage.

example: La télévision ne marche plus! Tu l'as **bousillée**!

as spoken: La télé~, è marche plus! Tu l'as **bousillée**!

translation: The television doesn't work anymore! You **broke** it!

carapater (se) *v.* to leave quickly, "to scram."

example: Voilà le patron! On **se carapate**!

as spoken: V'là l'patron! On **s'carapate**!

translation: There's the boss! Let's **beat it**!

casseur *m.* burglar • (lit); one who breaks things (such as windows in order to gain entry).

example: Le **casseur** a volé mon manteau neuf et tous mes diamants!

as spoken: Le **casseur**, l'a volé mon manteau neuf et tous mes diams!

translation: The **burglar** took my new coat and all my diamonds!

NOTE (1): **casser** *v.* to rob, to break in • (lit); to break.

NOTE (2): **diams** *m.pl.* a popular abbreviation for *diamants* meaning "diamonds."

cuisiner *v.* to interrogate, to pump or grill someone for information • (lit); to cook.

example: Les détectives ont **cuisiné** le casseur pendant trois heures.

as spoken: Les détectives, y z'ont **cuisiné** l'casseur pendant trois heures.

translation: The detectives **interrogated** the burglar for three hours.

écoper *v.* to receive something that is unwanted.

example: C'est toujours moi qui **écope**!

as spoken: [no change]

translation: I'm always the one who gets **blamed** for everything!

SYNONYM: **trinquer** *v.*

encarrer *v.* to enter.

example: La prochaine fois que tu **encarres** dans ma chambre sans permission, je te casse la gueule!

as spoken: La prochaine fois qu' t'**encarres** dans ma chamb' sans permission, j'te casse la gueule!

translation: The next time you **enter** my room without permission, I'll clobber you!

NOTE: As learned in lesson one, the feminine noun **gueule** (literally "the mouth of an animal") means "mug" or "mouth" in slang.

exact *adv.* a common abbreviation of *exactement* meaning "exactly" or "righto."

example: "Tu crois qu'il a volé la moto?"
"**Exact**!"

as spoken: [no change]

translation: "You think he stole the motorcycle?"
"**Exactly**!"

flicaille *f.* the police (in general).

example: Appelle la **flicaille**! Je crois qu'il y a un cambrioleur chez moi!

as spoken: Appelle la **flicaille**! J'crois qu'y a un casseur chez moi!

translation: Call the **police**! I think there's a burglar in my house!

NOTE: **casseur** *m.* (from the verb *casser* meaning "to break) burglar • (lit); one who breaks (in).

SYNONYM (2): **flic** *m. (extremely popular)* policeman, "cop."

SYNONYM (2): **poulet** *m.* • (lit); chicken.

SYNONYM (3): **motard** *m.* motorcycle-cop.

fourrer *v.* to cram, to stick.

example: Où tu as **fourré** mes clés? Ça fait une bonne heure que j'essaie de les trouver!

as spoken: Où t'as **fourré** mes clés? Ça fait une bonne heure qu' j'essaie d'les trouver!

translation: Where did you **stick** my keys? I've been looking for them for an entire hour!

histoire *v.* ordeal, "adventure" • (lit); story.

example: J'ai passé une heure au supermarché parce qu'il y avait un monde fou! Puis ça m'a pris deux heures pour rentrer à cause d'un accident sur la route. Quelle **histoire**!

as spoken: J'ai passé une heure au supermarché pasqu'y avait un monde fou! Puis ça m'a pris deux heures pour rentrer à cause d'un accident sur la route. Quelle **histoire**!

translation: I spent one hour at the supermarket because there was an enormous crowd! Then it took me two hours to get home because of an accident on the way. What an **ordeal**!

lessivé(e) (être) *adj.* to be exhausted • (lit); to be washed out.

example: Je suis **lessivé**. Je vais me coucher.

as spoken: J'suis **lessivé**. J'vais m'coucher.

translation: I'm **wiped out**. I'm going to bed.

SYNONYM (1): **claqué(e) (être)** *adj.* (*claquer* = to burst).

SYNONYM (2): **crevé(e) (être)** *adj.* (*crever* = to burst, to split).

SYNONYM (3): **esquinté(e) (être)** *adj.* (*esquinter* = to exhaust).

lourde *f.* door • (lit); that which is heavy.

example: Quand tu quittes la maison, il faut fermer la **lourde**.

as spoken: Quand tu quittes la maison, ~ faut fermer la **lourde**.

translation: When you leave the house, you have to close the **door**.

mec *m.* guy, "dude."

example: Tu connais ce **mec**-là? Je crois que c'est notre nouveau professeur d'anglais.

as spoken: Tu connais c'**mec**-là? J'crois qu'c'est not'nouveau prof~ d'anglais.

translation: Do you know that **guy**? I think that's our new English teacher.

mettre au clou *exp.* to hock • (lit); to hang on the nail.

example: Si tu as besoin de fric, **mets** ta guitare **au clou**.

as spoken: Si t'as b'soin d'fric, **mets** ta guitare **au clou**.

translation: If you need some money, **hock** your guitar.

pige *f.* year.

example: Le trois novembre, j'aurai trente **piges**.

as spoken: [no change]

translation: On November third, I'll be thirty **years** old.

piquer *v.* to steal, "swipe" • (lit); to prick or sting.

example: Arrêtez-le! Il a **piqué** mon vélo!

as spoken: Arrêtez-le! L'a **piqué** mon vélo!

translation: Stop him! He **stole** my bike!

SYNONYM: **barboter** *v.* • (lit); to paddle in mud or water.

placard *m.* jail • (lit); closet.

example: Le flic a mis le voleur au **placard**.

as spoken: Le flic, l'a mis l'voleur au l'**placard**.

translation: The cop put the thief in **jail**.

SYNONYMS: *(en) taule* • *(au) violon* • *(au) frais.*

planquer *v.* to hide.

example: Je dois **planquer** ce cadeau. C'est une surprise pour mon mari.

as spoken: J'dois **planquer** c'cadeau. C't'une surprise pour mon mari.

translation: I have **to hide** this present. It's a surprise for my husband.

NOTE (1): **planque** *f.* hiding place.

plumard *m.* bed • (lit); that which has feathers (from the feminin noun "*plume*" meaning "feather").

example: Mon **plumard** est trop mou!

as spoken: Mon **plumard**, l'est trop mou!

translation: My **bed** is too soft!

NOTE: **se plumarder** *v.* to go to bed.

SYNONYM: **pieu** *m.* *(aller au pieu).*

SYNONYM: **pieuter (se)** *v.* to go to bed.

probable *adv.* a common abbreviation of *probablement* meaning "probably."

example: "Je me demande pourquoi elle est partie si vite!"
"**Probable** qu'elle était en retard pour un meeting."

as spoken: "J'me d'mande pourquoi l'est partie si vite!"
"**Probab'** qu'elle était en r'tard pour un meeting."

translation: "I wonder why she left so quickly!"
"**Probably** because she was late for a meeting."

radiner *v.* to show up, to arrive.

example: Mon père était supposé **radiner** il y a une heure. Peut-être que la circulation était mauvaise ce soir.

as spoken: Mon père, l'était supposé **radiner** ~ y a une heure! P't-êt' que la circulation, l'était mauvaise ce soir.

translation: My father was supposed **to arrive** an hour ago! Maybe traffic was heavy tonight.

NOTE: Although the verb *arriver* is conjugated with *être*, its slang synonym **radiner** is conjugated with *avoir:*
Je suis arrivé = **J'ai radiné**.

salut *interj.* hi.

example: **Salut**, Carole! Henri m'a dit que tu as été très malade! J'espère que tu vas mieux maintenant.

as spoken: **Salut**, Carole! Henri, y m'a dit qu' t'as été très malade! J'espère que tu vas mieux maintenant.

translation: **Hi** Carole! Henry told me that you've been sick! I hope you're doing better now.

NOTE: **salut** is used to mean both "hi" and "good-bye" depending on the context.

SYNONYM: **ciao** *interj.* Borrowed from Italian, this interjection is used extensively by the French. Unlike *salut*, **ciao** only means "good-bye."

téloche *f.* television.

example: Mes parents viennent d'acheter une nouvelle **téloche**. Elle est énorme! Il faut que tu viennes la voir!

as spoken: Mes parents, y viennent d'acheter une nouvelle **téloche**. L'est énorme! ~Faut qu'tu viennes la voir!

translation: My parents just bought a new **television**. It's huge! You've got to come over and see it!

"Tu parles!" *exp.* **1.** "You said it!" • **2.** "You've gotta be kidding!"

example (1): "Léon est bizarre, lui!"
"**Tu parles**!"

as spoken: "Léon, l'est bizarre, lui!"
"**Tu parles**!

translation: "Léon is really strange!"
"**You said it**!"

example (2): "Julie est ta meilleure copine, n'est-ce pas?"
"**Tu parles**! Je ne l'aime pas du tout!"

as spoken: "Julie, c'est ta meilleure copine, n'est-c'pas?"
"**Tu parles**! J'l'aime pas du tout!"

translation: "Julie's your best friend, right?"
"**You've gotta be kidding**! I can't stand her!"

NOTE: **copain** *m.*/**copine** *f.* friend, pal.

VARIATION: **"Tu parles, Charles!"** • The French occasionally use a rhyming proper name after an expression for added effect. Example:

A la tienne, Etienne! = Here's to you!
Ça colle, Anatole? = How's it going?
Ça fait du bien, Adrien! = That feels great!
Comme de juste, Auguste! = You said it, Charley!

Practice the Vocabulary

[Answers to Lesson 3, p. 220]

A. Complete the phrases by choosing the appropriate word from the list below.

agrafer	**écopé**	**placard**
balader	**flicaille**	**planquer**
baraque	**fourré**	**plumard**
bousillé	**lourde**	**salut**

1. Le voleur, y s'est fait ________________ par les flics.
2. En entrant, l'a fermé la ________________ .
3. Suzanne, l'a __________________ un mois d'prison.
4. J'ai habité dans cette ____________________ toute ma vie.
5. On m'a __________________ en prison.
6. A plus tard. ________________ !
7. On a volé mon portefeuille! Appelle la __________________ !
8. J'suis vraiment fatigué. J'vais aller au ______________________ .
9. Quel temps splendide. J'ai envie d'me ____________________ .
10. Le flic, l'a mis l'voleur au ______________________ .
11. Qui a __________________ mon rasoir électrique? Y marche plus!
12. La police! Faut s'__________________ !

B. From the right column, choose the slang synonym of the words in parentheses by writing the corresponding number in the box.

☐ 1. J'suis *(très fatigué)* c'matin.

☐ 2. Y m'a *(interrogé)* pendant une heure!

☐ 3. Elle habite dans une grande *(maison)*.

☐ 4. Quel *(désordre)*!

☐ 5. Quand è va *(arriver)*?

☐ 6. J'ai 18 *(ans)* aujourd'hui.

☐ 7. A l'aéroport, j'ai oublié où j'avais garé la voiture. Enfin, j'l'ai trouvée deux heures après! Quelle *(aventure)*!

☐ 8. Le voleur, il *(est parti vite)*.

☐ 9. J'ai *(cassé)* l'téléphone quand j'l'ai fait tomber par accident.

☐ 10. Y fait beau aujourd'hui. J'pense que j'vais m'*(promener)* un peu.

A. **histoire**

B. **cuisiné**

C. **bordel**

D. **baraque**

E. **piges**

F. **balader**

G. **s'est carapaté**

H. **radiner**

I. **lessivé**

J. **bousillé**

C. Translate each sentence into French by replacing the italicized word(s) with the slang synonym shown in boldface.

(Make all necessary changes to the verbs. Always make sure to use contractions where appropriate.)

Example:

This is a beautiful house!
(**baraque**) **C't'une belle baraque!**

1. He *stole* my bike.
   (**piquer**) ______________________________.

2. I want to watch *T.V.*
   (**téloche**) ______________________________.

3. I *broke* my watch.
   (**bousiller**) ______________________________.

4. There's the *robber*!
   (**casseur**) ______________________________.

5. Do you want *to go in*?
   (**encarrer**) ______________________________?

6. You know that *guy*?
   (**mec**) ______________________________?

7. If you don't want your guitar anymore, you could *hock it*!
   (**la mettre au clou**) ______________________________.

8. What time did they *show up*?
   (**radiner**) ______________________________?

9. Do you want *to stroll* after dinner?
   (**se balader**) ______________________________?

10. I'm *pooped*!
    (**lessivé**) ______________________________!

A CLOSER LOOK:
The Structure of a Sentence

A. Subject followed by a personal pronoun

In the previous lesson, we learned how to construct a question in spoken French. The structure of a statement is equally important. In colloquial French, the subject is commonly followed by a personal pronoun such as: **il** (**y**), **elle**(**s**) (**è**), and **ils** (**y** or **z**). The verb then follows:

Cécile me fait toujours rire.
Cécile, è m'fait toujours rire.

Ce pantalon me va bien.
Ce pantalon, y m'va bien.

B. Subject/object at the end of a sentence

Another very popular construction is one in which the subject or object appears at the end of the sentence

SUBJECT

Cécile me fait toujours rire.
È m'fait toujours rire, Cécile.

Ce pantalon m'va bien.
Y m'va bien, c'pantalon.

OBJECT

Je vois Anne souvent.
J'la vois souvent, Anne.

T'as parlé à Jean hier?
Tu lui as parlé hier, à Jean?

C. Interrogative terms at the end of a phrase

The structure illustrated above (in which a complete sentence is formed first with the subject placed at the end) also applies to questions with the interrogative terms below:

combien, **comment**, **où**, **pourquoi**, **quand**, **quel(le)**, **qui** & **quoi**

As learned in Lesson 2, these interrogative terms (with the exception of **quoi**) can be placed at the beginning of a statement to transform it into a question:

Quand *tu dois partir?*
Comment *tu vas faire ça?*
Combien *elle en a, d'enfants?*

It is equally common to form a question by placing the interrogative term at the *end* of a statement:

Tu dois partir ***quand****?*
Tu vas faire ça ***comment****?*
Elle en a ***combien****, d'enfants?*

NOTE: In the previous example, **combien** ends the phrase with the object placed at the end for more emphasis:

She has how many of them...children (that is)?

EXERCISES

A. Practice personal pronouns.

Rewrite each sentence with (a) the appropriate personal pronoun after the subject and (b) the subject at the end.

Example:
Jean va bientôt arriver.
a) **Jean, y va bientôt arriver.**
b) **Y va bientôt arriver, Jean.**

1. Ce gâteau est délicieux.
   a. ______________________________.
   b. ______________________________.

2. Suzanne est très jolie.
   a. ______________________________.
   b. ______________________________.

3. Le dîner est gâché.
   a. ______________________________.
   b. ______________________________.

4. Cette robe me va comme un gant.

   a. ____.

   b. ____.

5. Le film était fantastique.

   a. ____.

   b. ____.

6. Ma mère m'appelle.

   a. ____.

   b. ____.

7. Les jours passent vite.

   a. ____.

   b. ____.

8. Cette voiture est toute neuve.

   a. ____.

   b. ____.

9. Mon frère est très grand.

   a. ____.

   b. ____.

10. Serge te demande au téléphone.

   a. ____.

   b. ____.

B. Rewrite the question.

Rewrite the question in French by: (1) replacing the italicized word(s) with the appropriate synonym from the list below and (2) placing the interrogative term toward the end of the phrase. Give the correct form of the verb.

Example:

What did he *throw* on the table?

(quoi) *Il a jeté quoi sur la table?*

baraque	**fourrer**	**radiner**
bordel	**lessivé**	**se balader**
bousiller	**piquer**	**se carapater**
flicaille	**planquer**	**téloche**

1. Why are you making this *mess*?

   (**pourquoi**) ______________________________?

2. What did you *break*?

   (**quoi**) ______________________________?

3. Which *house* are you going to buy?

   (**quelle**) ______________________________?

4. When did he *steal* it?

   (**quand**) ______________________________?

5. Whom are you trying *to hide*?

   (**qui**) ______________________________?

6. Why did you leave *quickly*?

   (**pourquoi**) ______________________________?

7. When is he going to talk to the *cops*?

   (**quand**) ______________________________?

8. How many *televisions* do you have?

   (**combien**) ____ ?

9. Whom did they *show up* with?

   (**qui**) ____ ?

10. Where are you going to go *stroll*?

    (**où**) ____ ?

11. Why are you *pooped*?

    (**pourquoi**) ____ ?

12. Who did they *throw* in prison?

    (**qui**) ____ ?

DICTATION
Test Your Aural Comprehension.

(This dictation can be found in Appendix A on page 236)

If you are following along with your cassette, you will now hear a paragraph containing many of the terms from this section. The paragraph will be read at normal conversational speed (which may actually seem fast to you at first). In addition, the words will be pronounced as you would actually hear them in a conversation, including many common reductions.

The first time the paragraph is presented, simply listen in order to get accustomed to the speed and heavy use of reductions. The paragraph will then be read again with a pause after each group of words to give you time to write down what you heard. The third time the paragraph is read, follow along with what you have written.

LEÇON QUATRE

La Joie d'Être *Bouchon*

(The joy of being the ***youngest****)*

(La Famille)

Leçon Quatre

Dialogue in slang

La Joie d'Être Bouchon

Daniel: Alors, elle était comment la grande réunion?

Richard: Au début, Je m'**en suis payé une tranche** mais pas vers la fin! Ma **vieille** et mon **vieux** se sont **bagarrés**!

Daniel: Ils se sont **bouffé le nez**, tes **vieux**, hein?

Richard: Tu parles! Pour commencer, ma **frangine s'est engueulée** avec mon **beauf** sans arrêt.

Daniel: Mais pourquoi?

Richard: Dès le commencement, ils étaient déjà **survoltés** parce que leur **fiston** et leur **fifille** ne faisaient que **chialer**!

Daniel: Mon **frangin** ne veut pas de **moutards** à cause de ça.

Richard: Alors, ma **tatie** a voulu **se mêler** mais mon **tonton** lui a dit que **ce n'était pas ses oignons**.

Daniel: Et les **beaux-vieux**...ils s'amusaient?

Richard: **Tu rigoles**! Ma **belle-doche** était **de mauvais poil** parce que mon **beau-dab** a **fait la gueule** toute la soirée!

Daniel: Ils ont l'air vraiment charmants!

Richard: Donc...j'ai passé la soirée à **faire l'**arbitre! Ah, la joie d'être **bouchon**!

Daniel: Si jamais je décide de **signer un bail**, j'espère que ma **régulière** n'aura pas une grande famille!

Leçon Quatre

Translation in English

Daniel: So, how was the big reunion?

Richard: In the beginning, I **had a great time** but not toward the end! My **mom** and **dad** really **blew up** at each other.

Daniel: Your **parents** really **got into it**, huh?

Richard: You're not kidding! To start off, my **sister** kept **chewing out** my **brother-in-law** nonstop.

Daniel: Why was that?

Richard: Right from the start, they were already **worked up** because their little **son** and **daughter** were doing nothing but **crying**!

Daniel: My **brother** doesn't want **kids** because of that.

Richard: So, my **aunt** wanted to intervene but my **uncle** told her that **it was none of her business**.

Daniel: What about the **in-laws**...did they have fun?

Richard: **You're kidding**! My **mother-in-law** was **in a lousy mood** because my **father-in-law** just **frowned** all evening!

Daniel: They sound truly charming!

Richard: So...I spent my evening **acting as** referee! Ah, the joy of being the **youngest**!

Daniel: If I ever decide to get **hitched**, I hope my **wife** doesn't have a big family!

Leçon Quatre

Dialogue in slang as it would be spoken

La Joie d'Êt' Bouchon

Daniel: Alors, l'était comment la grande réunion?

Richard: Au début, J'm'**en suis payé une tranche** mais pas vers la fin! Ma **vieille** et mon **vieux**, y se sont **bagarrés**!

Daniel: Y s'sont **bouffé l'nez**, tes **vieux**, hein?

Richard: Tu parles! Pour commencer, ma **frangine**, è **s'est engueulée** avec mon **beauf** sans arrêt.

Daniel: Mais pourquoi?

Richard: Dès l'commencement, y z'étaient déjà **survoltés** pasque leur **fiston** et leur **fifille**, y faisaient qu'**chialer**!

Daniel: Mon **frangin**, y veut pas d'**moutards** à cause de ça.

Richard: Alors, ma **tatie**, l'a voulu **s'mêler** mais mon **tonton**, y lui a dit qu'**c'était pas ses oignons**.

Daniel: Et les **beaux-vieux**...y s'amusaient?

Richard: **Tu rigoles**! Ma **belle-doche**, l'était **d'mauvais poil** pasqu'mon **beau-dab**, l'a **fait la gueule** toute la soirée!

Daniel: Z'ont l'air vraiment charmants!

Richard: Donc...j'ai passé la soirée à **faire** l'arbitre! Ah, la joie d'êt'**bouchon**!

Daniel: Si jamais j'décide de **signer un bail**, j'espère qu'ma **régulière**, l'aura pas une grande famille!

Vocabulary

bagarrer (se) *v.* to fight.

example: Arrêtez de vous **bagarrer** tout le temps!

as spoken: Arrêtez d'vous **bagarrer** tout l'temps!

translation: Stop **fighting** all the time!

NOTE: **bagarre** *f.* fight.

example: Tu as entendu la **bagarre** entre Marie et Jean?

as spoken: T'as entendu la **bagarre** entre Marie et Jean?

translation: Did you hear the **fight** between Marie and Jean?

ALSO: **chercher la bagarre** *exp.* to look for a fight.

SYNONYM: **se chamailler** *v.*

beauf *m.* brother-in-law.

example: Le frère de mon mari est mon **beauf**.

as spoken: Le frère d'mon mari, c'est mon **beauf**.

translation: The brother of my husband is my **brother-in-law**.

NOTE (1): **beauf** is a shortened version of "*beau-frère.*"

NOTE (1): **beauf** is also used to mean "average, mediocre, narrow-minded guy."

beau-dab *m.* father-in-law.

example: Le père de ma femme est mon **beau-dab**.

as spoken: Le père de ma femme, c'est mon **beau-dab**.

translation: The father of my wife is my **father-in-law**.

beaux-vieux *m.pl.* parents-in-law.

example: Les parents de mon mari sont mes **beaux-vieux**.

as spoken: Les parents d'mon mari, ce sont mes **beaux-vieux**.

translation: The parents of my husband are my **parents-in-law**.

belle-doche *f.* mother-in-law.

example: Ma **belle-doche** est une chipie!

as spoken: Ma **belle-doche**, c't'une chipie!

translation: My **mother-in-law** is a shrew!

bouchon *m.* the youngest member of the family • (lit); stopper, plug, cork (of a bottle).

example: Je suis le **bouchon** de la famille.

as spoken: J'suis l'**bouchon** d'la famille.

translation: I'm the **youngest member** of the family.

NOTE: The nonslang, academic replacement for *bouchon* is *benjamin(e)*.

bouffer le nez (se) *exp.* to fight • (lit); to eat each other's nose.

example: Pourquoi ils vivent toujours ensemble? Ils **se bouffent le nez** sans arrêt!

as spoken: Pourquoi y vivent toujours ensemble? Y **s'bouffent le nez** sans arrêt!

translation: Why do they still live together? They **fight** nonstop!

NOTE: This humorous expression describes two people yelling at each other so closely that they look at if they are eating each other's nose.

"Ce n'est pas tes oignons" *exp.* "It's none of your business" • (lit); "It's none of your onions."

example: "Combien tu pèses?"
"**Ce n'est pas tes oignons**!"

as spoken: "Combien tu pèses?"
"**C'est pas tes oignons**!"

translation: "How much do you weigh?"
"**It's none of your business**!"

SYNONYM: **"De quoi je me mêle?"** *exp.* • (lit); "What am I (you) getting into?"

chialer *v.* to cry (very popular).

example: Ce bébé-là **chiale** tout le temps!

as spoken: C'bébé-là, y **chiale** tout le temps!

translation: This baby **cries** all the time!

de mauvais poil (être) *exp.* to be in a bad mood • (lit); to have one's body hair bristle the wrong way.

example: Tu es **de mauvais poil** aujourd'hui! Qu'est-ce qu'il y a?

as spoken: T'es **d'mauvais poil** aujourd'hui! Qu'est-c'qu'y a?

translation: You're **in a bad mood** today! What's wrong?

ANTONYM: **de bon poil (être)** *exp.* to be in a good mood.

NOTE: **à poil (être)** *exp.* to be stark naked.

engueuler *v.* to yell (at someone).

example: Ma mère m'a **engueulé** pendant toute une heure parce que je suis rentré après minuit.

as spoken: Ma mère, è m'a **engueulé** pendant toute une heure pasque j'suis rentré après minuit.

translation: My mother **yelled** at me for an entire hour because I came home past midnight.

NOTE: This comes from the slang word **gueule** *f.* which is derogatory for "mouth." Therefore, **engueuler** might be literally translated as "to mouth off at (someone)."

ALSO: **s'engueuler avec quelqu'un** *exp.* to have a verbal fight with someone.

example: Marie **s'est engueulée avec** le patron!

as spoken: Marie, è **s'est engueulée avec** le patron!

translation: Marie **had words with** the boss!

faire la gueule *exp.* **1.** to pout, frown • **2.** to give the cold shoulder.

example (1): Ma petite sœur **fait la gueule** parce que mes parents lui ont donné une poupée pour son anniversaire, alors qu'elle voulait un vélo.

as spoken: Ma p'tite sœur, è **fait la gueule** pasque mes parents, y lui ont donné une poupée pour son anniversaire, alors qu'è voulait un vélo.

translation: My little sister is **pouting** because my parents gave her a doll for her birthday, while she wanted a bicycle.

example (2): Ça fait deux jours qu'Anne me **fait la gueule**.

as spoken: Ça fait deux jours qu'Anne, è m'**fait la gueule**.

translation: Anne's been giving me the **cold shoulder** for two days.

NOTE: The difference between definitions **1.** and **2.** depends on the context.

faire le/la *c.l.* to act like a • (lit); to make the.

example: Arrête de **faire l'**idiot!

as spoken: [no change]

translation: Stop **acting like an** idiot!

fifille *f.* daughter.

example: Tu connais la **fifille** à Nancy?

as spoken: [no change]

translation: Do you know Nancy's **daughter**?

SYNONYMS: **fillette** *f.* • **môme** *m.&f.* • **mouflette** *f.*

NOTE: Although the correct preposition is *de*, in slang and familiar French, it becomes *à*.

fiston *m.* son.

example: C'est ton **fiston**? Il te ressemble beaucoup.

as spoken: C'est ton **fiston**? Y t'ressemble beaucoup.

translation: That's your **son**? He looks a lot like you.

NOTE: **Fiston** is a slang transformation of "*fils.*"

SYNONYMS: **môme** *m.&f.* • **mouflet** *m.*

frangine *f.* sister.

example: Je ne savais pas que tu avais une **frangine**.

as spoken: J'savais pas qu' t'avais une **frangine**.

translation: I didn't know you had a **sister**.

frangin *m.* brother.

example: Je te présente Henri. C'est le **frangin** de Marcel.

as spoken: J'te présente Henri. C'est l'**frangin** à Marcel.

translation: I'd like you to meet Henri. He's Marcel's **brother**.

mêler (se) *v.* to interfere, to stick one's nose into someone's business • (lit); to mix, blend.

example: Ne te **mêle** pas de mes affaires!

as spoken: ~ te **mêle** pas de mes affaires!

translation: Don't **stick your nose** into my business!

moutards *m.pl.* kids.

example: Ma frangine travaille dans une école maternelle. Heureusement qu'elle adore les **moutards**!

as spoken: Ma frangine, è travaille dans une école maternelle. Heureusement qu'elle adore les **moutards**!

translation: My sister works in an elementary school. It's a good thing she loves **kids**!

SYNONYM (1): **mômes** *m.&f.pl* • **mioches** *m.&f.pl.* • **mouflets** *m.pl.*

payer une tranche (s'en) *exp.* to have a great time • (lit); to treat oneself to a slice of it ("it" signifying "fun").

example: On **s'en est payé une tranche** à la plage!

as spoken: [no change]

translation: What a **great time** we had at the beach!

NOTE: **se payer** *v.* to treat oneself.

régulière *f.* wife • (lit); legitimate one.

example: Ma **régulière** est présidente d'une grande compagnie à Paris.

as spoken: Ma **régulière**, l'est présidente d'une grande compagnie à Paris.

translation: My **wife** is the president of a big company in Paris.

NOTE (1): **bourgeoise** *f.* wife • (lit); middle-class woman.

NOTE (2): **légitime** *f.* • (lit); legitimate one.

signer un bail *v.* to get married • (lit); to sign a lease.

example: Ralph et Jacqueline vont **signer un bail** dans deux jours!

as spoken: Ralph et Jacqueline, y vont **signer un bail** dans deux jours!

translation: Ralph and Jacqueline are going **to get hitched** in two days!

survolté(e) (être) *exp.* to be all worked up • (lit); to be boosted up (in regards to electrical current).

example: Ne lui parle pas! Il est **survolté** aujourd'hui!

as spoken: ~ lui parle pas! L'est **survolté** aujourd'hui!

translation: Don't speak to him! He's **all worked up** today!

tatie *f.* aunt.

example: La sœur de ma mère est ma **tatie**.

as spoken: La sœur à ma mère, c'est ma **tatie**.

translation: My mother's sister is my **aunt**.

SYNONYM: **tantine** *f.*

tonton *m.* uncle.

example: Le frère de mon père est mon **tonton**.

as spoken: Le frère à mon père, c'est mon **tonton**.

translation: My father's brother is my **uncle**.

"Tu rigoles!" *exp.* "You're kidding!"

example: "Ce matin j'ai trouvé un diamant sur le trottoir!"
"Tu rigoles!"

as spoken: "C'matin j'ai trouvé un diam su'l'trottoir!"
"Tu rigoles"

translation: "This morning I found a diamond on the sidewalk!"
"**You're kidding**!"

vieille *f.* mother (disrespectful) • (lit); old lady.

example: C'est l'anniversaire de ma **vieille** aujourd'hui.

as spoken: C'est l'anniversaire d'ma **vieille** aujourd'hui.

translation: Today's my **mother**'s birthday.

SYNONYM: **vioque** *f.*

vieux *m.* father (disrespectful) • (lit); old man.

example: C'est ça ton **vieux**?

as spoken: [no change]

translation: Is that your **father**?

SYNONYM: **vioc** *m.*

vieux *m.pl.* parents (disrespectful) • (lit); old people, "old folks."

example: Mes **vieux** sont partis pour le Mexique pour un mois.

as spoken: Mes **vieux**, y sont partis pour le Mexique pour un mois.

translation: My **old folks** left for Mexico for a month.

SYNONYM (1): **viocs / vioques** *n.pl.*

SYNONYM (2): **dabs** *m.pl.*

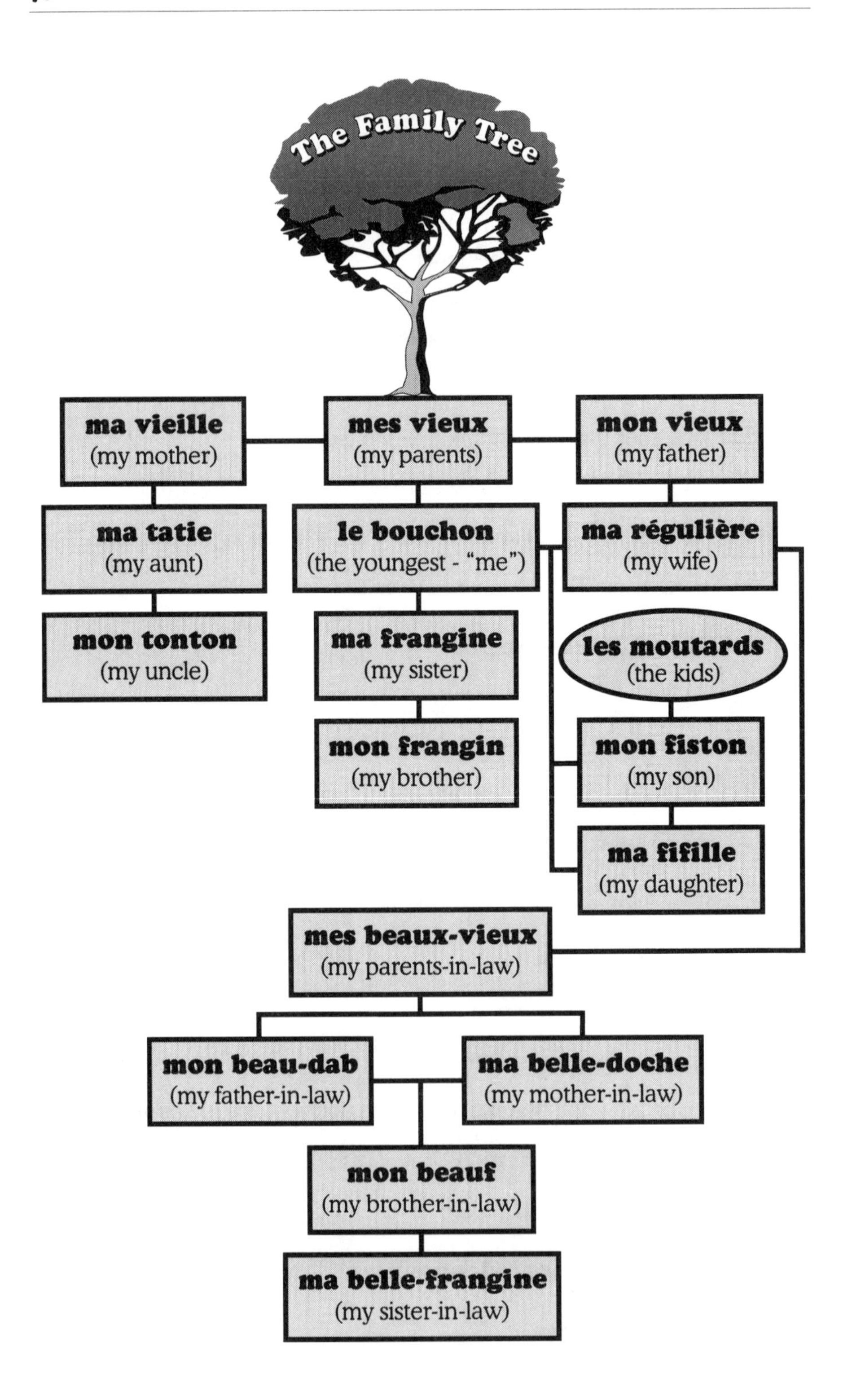
The Family Tree
ma vieille
(my mother)
mes vieux
(my parents)
mon vieux
(my father)
ma tatie
(my aunt)
le bouchon
(the youngest - "me")
ma régulière
(my wife)
mon tonton
(my uncle)
ma frangine
(my sister)
les moutards
(the kids)
mon frangin
(my brother)
mon fiston
(my son)
ma fifille
(my daughter)
mes beaux-vieux
(my parents-in-law)
mon beau-dab
(my father-in-law)
ma belle-doche
(my mother-in-law)
mon beauf
(my brother-in-law)
ma belle-frangine
(my sister-in-law)

Practice the Vocabulary 

[Answers to Lesson 4, p. 222]

A. Match the English with the French slang translation.

☐ 1. It's none of your business.

☐ 2. You're kidding!

☐ 3. I'd like you to meet my wife.

☐ 4. They fight all the time.

☐ 5. He's in a bad mood.

☐ 6. She acts innocent.

☐ 7. What a fight!

☐ 8. I had a fight with my best friend.

☐ 9. They do nothing but cry.

☐ 10. Why are you frowning?

☐ 11. We're having a great time here.

☐ 12. What are you all worked up about?

☐ 13. He's going to get married today.

A. On **s'en paie une tranche**, ici.

B. Je m'suis **engueulé** avec mon meilleur ami.

C. **C'est pas tes oignons**.

D. Pourquoi tu **fais la gueule**?

E. Y va **signer un bail** aujourd'hui.

F. J'te présente ma **régulière**.

G. Tu **rigoles**!

H. Y font qu'**chialer**.

I. Pourquoi t'es **survolté**?

J. L'est **d'mauvais poil**.

K. È **fait l'**innocente.

L. Quelle **bagarre**!

M. Y **s'bouffent le nez** tout l'temps.

B. Underline the synonym.

1. **bouchon**:
   a. benjamin b. aîné c. enfant

2. **fifille**:
   a. fils b. frère c. fille

3. **moutards**:
   a. mères b. cadets c. enfants

4. **frangin**:
   a. père b. frère c. fille

5. **vieux**:
   a. frère b. père c. fils

6. **fiston**:
   a. fils b. neveu c. enfant

7. **frangine**:
   a. sœur b. mère c. tante

8. **vieille**:
   a. mère b. tante c. sœur

9. **beauf**:
   a. frère b. beau-frère c. belle-sœur

10. **beaux-vieux**:
    a. beaux-parents b. beaux-frères c. oncles

11. **beau-dab**:
    a. beau-père b. beau-frère c. cadet

C. Complete the family tree by using the list below as a reference.

beau-dab	**fiston**	**tatie**
beauf	**fifille**	**tonton**
beaux-vieux	**frangin**	**vieille**
belle-doche	**frangine**	**vieux**
belle-frangine	**moutards**	**vieux**
bouchon	**régulière**	

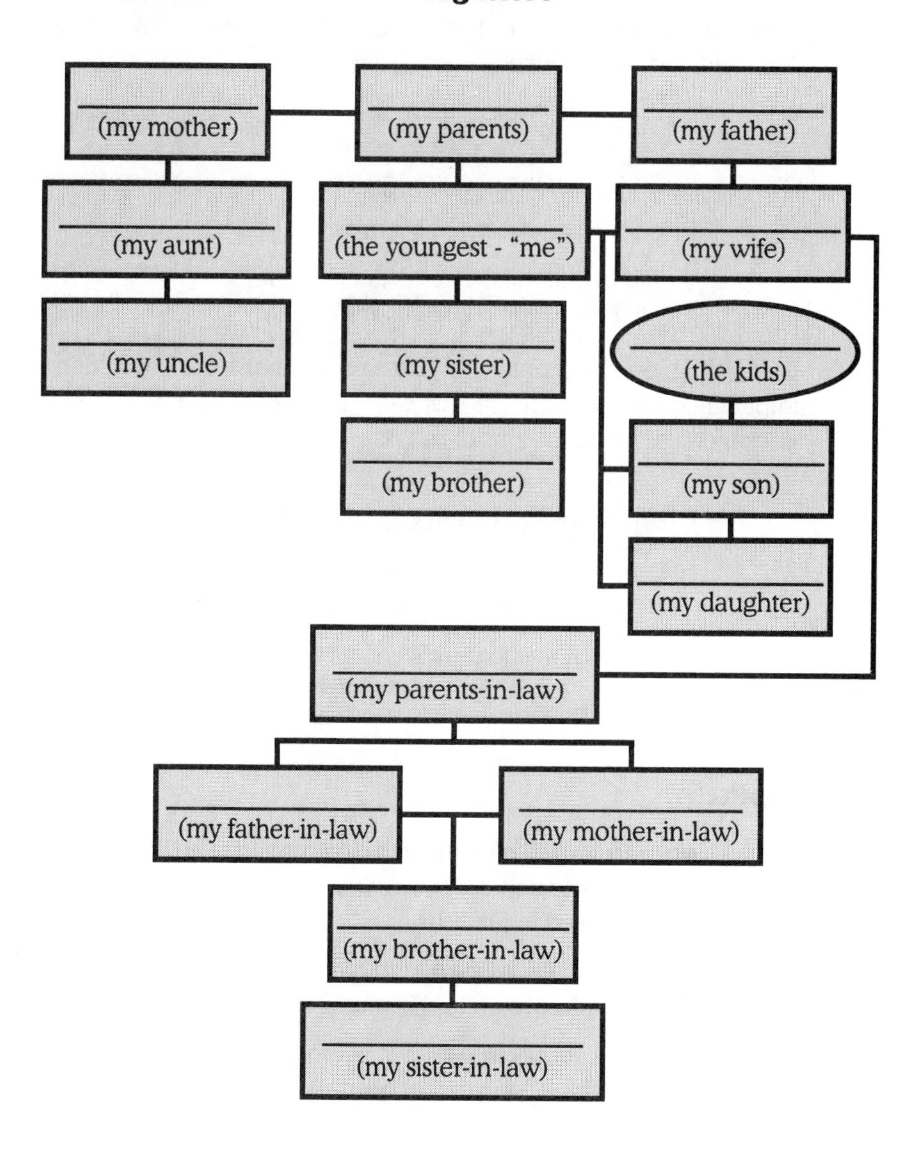

A CLOSER LOOK:
Words that Add Emphasis

A. "cette" = *c'te*
"ce" = *c'*
"cet" = *c't'*

1. Very often in daily conversation the demonstrative adjectives "*cette,*" "*ce,*" and "*cet*" are reduced:

   Regarde cette maison!
   *Regarde **c'te** maison!*

   Il est délicieux, ce gâteau!
   *Il est délicieux, **c'**gâteau!*

   Il a beaucoup d'énergie, cet enfant.
   *Il a beaucoup d'énergie, **c't'**enfant.*

2. Depending on the context, these abbreviations can also denote impatience or contempt. In this case, ***c'te***, ***c'***, and ***c't'*** become a package-deal meaning "this darn...".

   *J'en ai marre de **c'te** voiture!*
   (I'm fed up with this "darn" car!)

   *Quel crétin, **c'**mec!*
   (What a cretin, this "darn" guy is!)

   *Il m'énerve, **c't'**enfant!*
   (This "darn" kid is bugging me!)

B. un peu

The adverb ***un peu*** is used *after* the verb to emphasize an imperative or command. It is used in much the same way as demonstrative adjectives ("this" or "that") are used in English:

*Ecoute **un peu** la musique!*
(Just listen to this music!)

*Regarde **un peu** c'te maison!*
(Just look at that house!)

C. ben

1. The adverb ***ben***, pronounced like the French word "*bain*," is an extremely popular form of "*bien.*" However, ***ben*** is very frequently used like the emphatic "*mais*" to emphasize a question, a statement, or an imperative:

QUESTION
Mais où tu vas?
Ben *où tu vas?*

STATEMENT
Mais elle est très gentille!
Ben *elle est très gentille!*

IMPERATIVE
Mais regarde!
Ben *regarde!*

Unlike ***un peu***, ***ben*** always *precedes* the verb in the imperative form:

Regarde ***un peu****!*
Ben *regarde!*

2. In the imperative form, ***ben*** may be used with ***un peu*** to add a greater emphasis:

Ben *regarde* ***un peu****!*
Ben *arrête* ***un peu****!*

3. ***Ben*** is also frequently used to emphasize "oui" and "non." However, when used with "non," the interjection ***eh*** precedes ***ben***:

Y t'plaît comme professeur?	*C'est ton bébé?*
Ben *oui!*	***Eh, ben*** *non!*

4. The interjection ***eh*** may also be used with ***ben*** to create the exclamation ***Eh ben!*** meaning "Wow!" or "Gee!":

Nélie, l'a plaqué son mari?! ***Eh ben****!*
Nelie jilted her husband?! Wow!

NOTE: ***Ben*** is also used to mean "so":

Eh ***ben****?* (So?)
Ben *quoi?* (So what?)

D. donc

The conjunction ***donc*** is often used to emphasize a question or an imperative:

QUESTION

Pourquoi tu pars ***donc****?*
Où tu vas ***donc****?*

IMPERATIVE

Viens ***donc****!*
Arrête ***donc****!*

NOTE: In the imperative form, ***donc*** may be used together with **ben** to add even greater emphasis:

Ben *arrête* ***donc****!*
Ben *fais-le* ***donc****!*

E. alors

1. The adverb alors is commonly used to emphasize an interjection:

INTERJECTION

Quelle chance ***alors****!*
Fantastique ***alors****!*

2. **Alors** is also used to emphasize "*oui*" and "*non.*" Unlike **ben**, **alors** follows "*oui*" and "*non:*"

Y t'plaît comme prof?
Oui, ***alors****!*

C'est ton bébé?
Non, ***alors****!*

3. ***Alors*** is also very often used with ***ben*** (and ***eh, ben***) to add even stronger emphasis to "*oui*" and "*non:*"

Ben *oui,* ***alors****!*
(Well yes!)
Eh, ben *non,* ***alors****!*
(Well no!)

NOTE (1): ***Ben alors****?!* = So?!

NOTE (2): ***Ça alors!*** is an idiomatic expression meaning "Wow!"

Practice c'te, un peu, ben, & alors

A. Rewrite the following by using the word(s) in parentheses to add emphasis to the phrase.

Example:

Regarde cette robe!
(c'te) ***Regarde c'te robe!***

1. Ecoute cette musique!
   (un peu) ______________________________ !

2. Ecoute cette musique!
   (c'te) ______________________________ !

3. Ecoute cette musique!
   (un peu/c'te) ______________________________ !

4. Ecoute!
   (ben) ______________________________ !

5. Ecoute!
   (donc) ______________________________ !

6. Oui!
   (ben) ______________________ !

7. Oui!
   (alors) ______________________ !

8. Oui!
   (ben/alors) ______________________ !

9. Regarde cette architecture!
   (c't') ______________________ !

10. Regarde ce livre!
    (un peu) ______________________________!

11. Regarde ce livre!
    (un peu/c') __________________________!

12. Cours!
    (donc) ________________________!

13. Viens!
    (ben/donc) ____________________!

14. Regarde cette baraque!
    (ben/un peu/c'te) ____!

B. Fill in the blank using one of the following: *c'te • c' • c't' • un peu • ben • donc • alors.*

(There is one slang word in each sentence below from the dialogue. Can you recognize it?)

1. Tu crois qu'elle est belle? Oui ____________!
2. ____________ pourquoi tu fais la gueule?
3. Eh, ____________ non! C'est pas tes oignons!
4. Regarde ____________ces moutards! Y sont adorables!
5. Tu t'es engueulé avec ton beauf? __________non __________!
6. J'en ai marre de ____________bagarre!
7. ____________ ferme ____________ porte!
8. Je hais ____________cours de géométrie!

DICTATION

Test Your Aural Comprehension.

(This dictation can be found in Appendix A on page 237)

If you are following along with your cassette, you will now hear a paragraph containing many of the terms from this section. The paragraph will be read at normal conversational speed (which may actually seem fast to you at first). In addition, the words will be pronounced as you would actually hear them in a conversation, including many common reductions.

The first time the paragraph is presented, simply listen in order to get accustomed to the speed and heavy use of reductions. The paragraph will then be read again with a pause after each group of words to give you time to write down what you heard. The third time the paragraph is read, follow along with what you have written.

LEÇON CINQ

La Grande *Boum*

*(The big **bash**)*

(Une Soirée)

Leçon Cinq

Dialogue in slang

La Grande Boum

Marc: C'est **chouette**, cette **boum**!

Paul: Mais **mate** un peu comme ils sont tous bien **fringués**! Et moi qui ai l'air d'un **clodo**!

Marc: Ben pourquoi tu **te fais de la bile**? Tu es très bien comme ça. Tiens! Cette **nana**-là te **bigle**! Peut-être qu'elle **en pince pour toi**! Va la **brancher**!

Paul: **Rien à chiquer**! J'aurais la **trouille**.

Marc: Tu **déjantes**! Tu n'es pas venu pour **draguer**? Ben écoute! Je crois que tu as besoin de t'**en jeter un derrière la cravate** comme moi. C'est moi qui paie la première **tournée**.

Paul: Tu as **perdu la boule**! Tu veux me voir **tomber dans les pommes**? Si je m'**humectais les amygdales** avec ce **tord-boyaux** que tu as dans la **pince**, je serais **rond comme une queue de billard**.

Marc: Alors, si tu as soif, tu peux toujours **grenouiller**.

Paul: Tu sais, ce n'est pas **marrant**. Tout le monde ici parade avec une **clope** à la **gueule**. La fumée **schlingue**! Je vais avoir mal à la **gargue** si je reste ici.

Marc: J'ai l'impression que tu n'es pas fait pour les soirées, **mon vieux**!

Lesson Five

Translation in English

Marc: This **party** is really **great**!

Paul: But **get a load** how **decked out** everyone is! And me who look like a **slob**!

Marc: What are you **getting all worked up for**? You look fine. Hey! That **girl** over there is **giving you the eye**. Maybe she's **got a crush on you**! Go **talk** to her!

Paul: **No way**! I'd be **scared to death**!

Marc: You've **flipped**! Didn't you come here to **cruise**? Listen! I think you need **to get yourself something to drink** like me. I'll pay the first **round**.

Paul: You've **lost it**! Do you want to see me **pass out**? If I **downed** that **rot-gut** that you've got in your **hand**, I'd get **totally wasted**.

Marc: So, if you're thirsty, you can always **drink water**.

Paul: You know, it's not even **funny**. Everyone here is parading around with a **cigarette** in their **mouth**. Smoke **stinks**! I'm gonna get a sore **throat** if I stay here.

Marc: I have a feeling that you're just not cut out for parties, **pal**!

Leçon Cinq

Dialogue in slang as it would be spoken

La Grande Boum

Marc: C'est **chouette**, c'te **boum**!

Paul: Mais **mate** un peu comme y sont tous bien **fringués**! Et moi qu'ai l'air d'un **clodo**!

Marc: Ben pourquoi tu **t'fais d'la bile**? T'es très bien comme ça. Tiens! C'te **nana**-là, è t'**bigle**! P't'êt'qu'elle **en pince pour toi**! Va la **brancher**!

Paul: **Rien à chiquer**! J'aurais la **trouille**.

Marc: Tu **déjantes**! T'es pas v'nu pour **draguer**? Ben écoute! J'crois qu't'as b'soin d't'**en j'ter un derrière la cravate** comme moi. C'est moi qui paie la première **tournée**.

Paul: T'as **perdu la boule**! Tu veux m'voir **tomber dans les pommes**? Si j'm'**humectais les amygdales** avec ce **tord-boyaux** qu't'as dans la **pince**, je s'rais **rond comme une queue d'billard**.

Marc: Alors, si t'as soif, tu peux toujours **grenouiller**.

Paul: Tu sais, c'est pas **marrant**. Tout l'monde ici parade avec une **clope** à la **gueule**. La fumée, ça **schlingue**! J'vais avoir mal à la **gargue** si j'reste ici.

Marc: J'ai l'impression qu't'es pas fait pour les soirées, **mon vieux**!

Vocabulary

bigler *v.* to look from the corner of one's eye.

example: Je crois qu'elle te **bigle**.

as spoken: J'crois qu'è t'**bigle**.

translation: I think she's **looking** at you.

SYNONYM (1): **viser** *v.* • (lit); to aim (at someone or something).

SYNONYM (2): **reluquer** *v.* to eye someone or something.

boum *f.* big party, "a bash."

example: Demain je donne une **boum** chez moi. Je t'invite!

as spoken: Demain j'donne une **boum** chez moi. J't'invite!

translation: Tomorrrow I'm having a **party** at my house. You're invited!

brancher *v.* to talk to someone • (lit); to plug into.

example: Tiens! Voilà Richard! Je vais le **brancher**.

as spoken: Tiens! V'là Richard! J'vais l'**brancher**.

translation: Hey! There's Richard! I'm going **to talk** with him.

chouette *interj. (extremely popular)* terrific, neat • (lit); owl.

example: Ta maison est super **chouette**!

as spoken: L'est super **chouette**, ta maison!

translation: Your house is really **cool**!

clodo *m.* tramp, hobo, bum.

example: Change ta chemise, à la fin! Tu as l'air d'un vrai **clodo**!

as spoken: Change ta ch'mise, à la fin! T'as l'air d'un vrai **clodo**!

translation: Change your shirt already! You look like a real **bum**!

SYNONYM: **clochard** *m.*

clope *f. (extremely popular)* cigarette.

example: Tu peux me filer une **clope**?

as spoken: Tu peux m'filer une **clope**?

translation: Can you lend me a **cigarette**?

déjanter *v.* • **1.** to talk nonsense • **2.** to go crazy.

example (1): Ta grand-mère sait piloter un avion?! Mais, tu **déjantes**, toi!

as spoken: Ta grand-mère, è sait piloter un avion?! Mais, tu **déjantes**, toi!

translation: Your grand-mother can fly an airplane?! You're **crazy**!

example (2): Cette dame-là parle toute seule depuis une heure. Je crois qu'elle **déjante**!

as spoken: Cette dame-là, è parle toute seule depuis une heure. J'crois qu'è **déjante**!

translation: That woman over there has been talking to herself for an hour. I think she's **going crazy**.

SYNONYM: **déménager** *v.* • (lit); to move out (of own's mind).

draguer *v.* to cruise (for flirting or romantic encounters).

example: Tu vois la fille de l'autre côté de la salle? Je crois qu'elle te **drague**.

as spoken: Tu vois la fille d'l'aut' côté d'la salle? J'crois qu'è te **drague**.

translation: See that girl at the other side of the room? I think she's **cruising** you.

faire de la bile (se) *exp.* to get all worked up, to worry • (lit); to produce bile.

example: **Ne te fais pas de bile**. Je suis sûr qu'elle arrivera bientôt!

as spoken: **~ te fais pas d'bile**. J'suis sûr qu'elle arriv'ra bientôt!

translation: **Don't worry**. I'm sure she'll be here soon!

fringué(e) (être mal/bien) *adj.* to be poorly/well dressed.

example: Maurice est toujours **mal fringué**. Je crois que je vais lui offrir un joli pullover pour son anniversaire.

as spoken: Maurice, l'est toujours **mal fringué**. J'crois que j'vais lui offrir un joli pull~ pour son anniversaire.

translation: Maurice is always so **poorly dressed**. I think I'll give him a nice sweater for his birthday.

NOTE (1): **fringues** *f.pl.* clothes, "threads."

NOTE (2) **nippes** *f.pl.* clothes, "threads."

SYNONYM (1): **être mal/bien ficelé(e)** *exp.* • (lit); to be poorly/well strung (together).

SYNONYM (2): **être mal/bien nippé(e)** *exp.*

gargue *f.* throat.

example: Hier, j'ai hurlé pendant trois heures au match de football. Aujourd'hui, j'ai mal à la **gargue**.

as spoken: [no change]

translation: Yesterday, I yelled for three hours during the soccer game. Today, I have a sore **throat**.

NOTE: This comes from the verb **se gargariser** meaning "to gargle."

grenouiller *v.* to drink water • (lit); to do like a frog.

example: J'ai la gargue sèche. Je crois qu'il est temps de **grenouiller**.

as spoken: J'ai la gargue sèche. J'crois qu'il est temps d'**grenouiller**.

translation: My throat is dry. I think it's time **to have some water**.

NOTE: This comes from the feminine noun **grenouille** meaning "frog."

gueule *f.* mouth or face (depending on the context) • (lit); mouth of an animal.

example: Le ski ne m'intéresse pas du tout. Je n'ai pas envie de me casser la **gueule**!

as spoken: Le ski, ça ~ m'intéresse pas du tout. J'ai pas envie d'me casser la **gueule**!

translation: Skiing doesn't interest me at all. I don't feel like breaking my neck (or literally, **mouth** or **face**)!

NOTE: **se casser la gueule** *exp. (extremely popular)* to break one's neck • (lit); to break one's mouth or face.

SEE: **gueuleton**, *p. 8.*

ALSO: **emporter la gueule** *exp.* said of a something strong (peppers, hot mustard, etc.) that takes the roof off one's mouth, to pack a punch.

humecter les amygdales (s') *exp.* to drink, "to wet one's whistle" • (lit); to moisten one's tonsils.

example: Qu'est-ce que j'ai soif! Je vais **m'humecter les amygdales**.

as spoken: Qu'est-c'que j'ai soif! J'vais **m'humecter les amygdales**.

translation: Am I ever thirsty! I'm going **to go wet my whistle**.

jeter un derrière la cravate (s'en) *exp.* to drink • (lit); to throw one (a drink) behind one's tie.

example: Je crois que le patron **s'en jette un derrière la cravate** pendant le boulot.

as spoken: J'crois que l'patron, y **s'en jette un derrière la cravate** pendant le boulot.

translation: I think the boss **drinks** on the job.

NOTE: **boulot** *m. (extremely popular)* job, work.

marrant(e) *adj.* funny.

example: Cette comédienne est **marrante**! Personne ne me fait rire comme elle!

as spoken: L'est **marrante**, c'te comédienne! Personne ~ m'fait rire comme elle!

translation: That comedienne is so **funny**! No one makes me laugh like her!

NOTE (1): **Pas marrant(e)** is used to describe something which is very unpleasant or "a real drag."

NOTE (2): **se marrer** *v.* **1.** to laugh • **2.** to have a great time.

mater *v.* to look.

example: **Mate** ça! Je n'ai jamais rien vu de pareil dans toute ma vie!

as spoken: **Mate**-moi ça! J'ai jamais rien vu d'pareil dans toute ma vie!

translation: **Look** at that! I've never seen anything like it in my entire life!

NOTE: *moi* is commonly used to add emphasis to certain commands and interjections. See: *A Closer Look, p. 147*

nana *f. (extremely popular)* girl, "chick."

example: Elle s'appelle comment, cette **nana**? C'est la première fois que je la vois ici.

as spoken: È s'appelle comment, c'te **nana**? C'est la première fois qu'j'la vois ici.

translation: What's that **girl**'s name? This is the first time I've seen her here.

SYNONYM: **nénette** *f.*

ANTONYM: **mec** *m.* guy, "dude."

perdre la boule *exp.* to lose one's mind, "to lose it" • (lit); to lose the ball.

example: Tu ne sais pas ce que tu as fait de tes clés? C'est la troisième fois en deux jours que ça t'arrive! Je crois que tu commences à **perdre la boule**.

as spoken: Tu ~ sais pas c'que t'as fait d'tes clés? C'est la troisième fois en deux jours qu' ça t'arrive! J'crois qu' tu commences à **perd' la boule**.

translation: You don't know what you did with your keys? That's the third time in two days that's happened to you! I think you're starting **to lose it**.

pince *f.* hand • (lit); pincher (from the verb *pincer* meaning "to pinch").

example: Tu peux me donner un coup de **pince**?

as spoken: Tu peux m'donner un coup d'**pince**?

translation: Can you give me a **hand**?

SYNONYM: **paluche** *f.*

pincer pour quelqu'un (en) *exp.* to have a crush on someone.

example: Cette fille-là te regarde. Je crois qu'elle **en pince pour toi**!

as spoken: C'te fille-là, è t'regarde. J'crois qu'elle **en pince pour toi**!

translation: That girl over there is looking at you. I think she has a **crush on you**!

rien à chiquer *exp.* nothing doing, "No way, José!" • (lit); no tobacco.

example: Tu veux que je te prête mille balles? **Rien à chiquer**! Tu me dois toujours mille francs de la semaine dernière!

as spoken: Tu veux qu' j'te prête mille balles? **Rien à chiquer**! Tu m'dois toujours mille francs d'la s'maine dernière!

translation: You want me to lend you a thousand francs? **No way**! You still owe me a thousand francs from last week!

NOTE: The verb **chiquer** literally means "to chew tobacco."

rond(e) comme une queue de billard (être) *exp.* to be roaring drunk • (lit); to be round like a billiard cue.

example: Tu ne peux pas conduire! Tu es **rond comme une queue de billard**!

as spoken: Tu ~ peux pas conduire! T'es **rond comme une queue d'billard**!

translation: You can't drive! You're **wasted**!

NOTE: This expression is a play on words since the French word **rond(e)** is used to mean "drunk."

VARIATION: **rond(e) comme un manche de pelle (être)** *exp.* • (lit); to be round like a shovel handle.

schlinguer *v.* to stink.

example: Ça **schlingue** dans cette maison!

as spoken: Ça **schlingue** dans c'te maison!

translation: It **stinks** in this house!

NOTE: Also spelled **chlinguer**.

VARIATION: **schlingoter** *v.*

tomber dans les pommes *exp.* to faint, to pass out • (lit); to fall into the apples.

example: Quand Nancy a vu le spectre, elle est **tombée dans les pommes**!

as spoken: Quand Nancy, l'a vu l'spectre, l'est **tombée dans les pommes**!

translation: When Nancy saw the ghost, she **passed out**!

tord-boyaux *m.* very strong alcohol, "rot-gut" • (lit); gut-twister.

example: Mais comment tu arrives à descendre ce **tord-boyaux**?!

as spoken: Mais comment t'arrives à descend' ce **tord-boyaux**?!

translation: How can you down that **rot-gut**?

tournée *c.l.* round (of drinks) • (lit); a tour.

example: Je paie la première **tournée**, moi, si tu paies la seconde. D'accord?

as spoken: J'paie la première **tournée**, moi, si tu paies la z'gonde. D'acc~?

translation: I'll pay for the first **round** if you pay for the second. Okay?

NOTE: **payer/offrir une tournée** is a popular expression meaning "to treat to a round of drinks."

trouille (avoir la) *exp.* to be scared to death.

example: J'ai eu **la trouille** durant le tremblement de terre!

as spoken: J'ai eu **la trouille** durant l'tremblement d'terre!

translation: I was **scared to death** during the earthquake!

SYNONYM: **les jetons (avoir les)** *exp.* to be scared, to have the jitters • (lit); to have tokens.

vieux (mon) *c.l.* • **1.** my pal, my ol' buddy • **2.** my father, my old man.

example (1): Salut, **mon vieux**! Ça va?

as spoken: [no change]

translation: Hi, **pal**! How's everything going?

example (2): Je vais demander à **mon vieux** s'il peut me prêter sa bagnole.

as spoken: J'vais d'mander à **mon vieux** s'y peut m'prêter sa bagnole.

translation: I'll ask **my old man** if he'll lend me his car.

NOTE: **bagnole** *f. (extremely popular)* car.

SEE: **vieux** *m.* / **vieux** *m.pl. - p. 75.*

Practice the Vocabulary 

[Answers to Lesson 5, p. 223]

A. Complete the phrase by filling in the blank with the appropriate word from the list. Give the correct form of the verb.

bigler	**brancher**	**marrant**
bile	**clope**	**nana**
boule	**déjanter**	**schlinguer**
boum	**fringué**	**trouille**

1. J'ai envie d'fumer. Passe-moi une ______________ s'te plaît.

2. Ben, tu peux pas entrer comme ça! T'es mal ______________ !

3. J'veux rencontrer c'te __________ . J'vais la ______________ .

4. T'as perdu la ________________ , non? Tu peux pas l'faire!

5. L'est ________________ c'mec! Y m'fait toujours rire!

6. J'avais la ________________ quand j'ai fait ma présentation en classe.

7. J'suis nerveux pasqu'è m'______________ de l'aut'côté d'la classe.

8. Oh, ça ________________ dans c'te poissonnerie!

9. Mais quelle histoire! Tu ________________ , non?

10. Calme-toi! Pourquoi tu t'fais d'la ______________ ?

11. On s'est bien marré à la ________________ .

B. Underline the word that goes with the phrase.

1. L'a pas d'fric, lui. C't'un (**tord-boyaux**, **beauf**, **clodo**).

2. J'ai soif. J'vais m'en (**piquer**, **parler**, **jeter**) un derrière la cravate.

3. C't alcool, l'est trop fort! Quel tord-(**bras**, **boyaux**, **bouche**)!

4. Regarde un peu c't ivrogne. L'est (**riche**, **carré**, **rond**) comme une queue d'billard.

5. Y fait chaud dehors! J'vais m'humecter les (**amygdales**, **oreilles**, **pieds**).

6. J'sais pas comment tu arrives à fumer c'te (**porte**, **téloche**, **clope**). Ça schlingue!

7. Quand j'ai vu l'casseur dans la baraque, j'suis tombé dans les (**poires**, **pommes**, **pêches**).

8. J'aimerais bien la rencontrer. J'vais la (**brûler**, **brancher**, **brosser**).

9. L'est beau c'mec! J'en (**pince**, **prie**, **cours**) pour lui.

10. J'ai eu la (**truite**, **boue**, **trouille**) quand l'chien, l'a essayé d'm'attaquer!

11. L'est belle, c'te fille! J'vais la (**droguer**, **draguer**, **tirer**).

12. Quelle comédie (**trouille**, **pébroc**, **marrante**)!

13. J'ai trop fumé. Maintenant, j'ai mal à la (**gargouille**, **gargue**, **gare**).

C. Choose the slang synonym of the italicized word(s) by filling in the box with the corresponding letter.

☐ 1. L'est *fantastique*, c'film.

☐ 2. J'vais *m'évanouir* si j'mange pas tout d'suite!

☐ 3. J'aimerais bien prend' une bière, mais comme j'dois conduire, j'vais *boire de l'eau*.

☐ 4. T'as toujours une *cigarette* dans la bouche.

☐ 5. J'ai soif. J'ai b'soin d'me mett' de la flotte dans la *bouche*.

☐ 6. *Rien à faire*!

☐ 7. Comment ça va, mon *ami*?

☐ 8. Quand j'l'ai rencontré, y m'a serré la *main*.

☐ 9. Y passe son temps à regarder la *télévision*.

☐ 10. J'*suis amoureux de* ma prof de français.

☐ 11. Pourquoi t'es pas encore *habillé*?

☐ 12. J'avais *très peur*, moi!

A. **chouette**

B. **clope**

C. **en pince pour**

D. **gueule**

E. **grenouiller**

F. **la trouille**

G. **fringué**

H. **pince**

I. **rien à chiquer**

J. **téloche**

K. **tomber dans les pommes**

M. **vieux**

A CLOSER LOOK:

Popular Usage of Objective Case Personal Pronouns and " Ça"

A. Objective case personal pronouns

The student of French has no doubt learned how to emphasize the subject of a sentence with the use of the personal pronouns **moi**, **toi**, **lui**, **elle**, **nous**, **vous**, **eux**, and **elles**, and the demonstrative pronoun **ça**.

Je m'appelle David
Moi, *je m'appelle David.*

Tu es très amusant.
Toi, *tu es très amusant.*

Il est gentil.
Lui, *il est gentil.*

C'est fantastique!
Ça, *c'est fantastique!*

However, in colloquial French, these pronouns finish the statement. This construction is extremely popular:

Je m'appelle David, ***moi***.
Tu es très amusant, ***toi***.
Il est gentil, ***lui***.
C'est fantastique, ***ça***!

B. Further popular use of "ça"

The demonstrative pronoun **ça** is frequently used to emphasize the interrogative terms **comment**, **où**, **pourquoi**, **quand**, and **qui**. This is a very common usage of **ça**:

Regarde qui s'approche de nous!
Qui ça? (Who?)

J'vais y aller à midi.
Où ça? (Where to?)

EXERCISES

A. Practice Personal/Demonstrative Pronouns.

Emphasize the subject by adding the appropriate personal or demonstrative pronoun to the sentence. Choose from the list below.

moi • toi • lui • elle • nous • vous • eux • elles • ça

Example:
T'es en retard.
T'es en retard, **toi**.

1. J'suis fatigué, _________ .

2. L'est grand _________ .

3. È court vite, _________ .

4. Tu joues bien du piano, _________ .

5. Vous arrivez toujours en retard, _________ .

6. Pourquoi tu pleures, _________ ?

7. J'ai gagné l'grand prix, _________ !

8. L'est charmant, _________ .

9. È parle trois langues, _________ .

10. C'est bien, _________ .

11. Nous voilà arrivés, _________ !

12. C'est parfait, _________ !

B. RESPOND TO THE STATEMENT

Respond to each statement by using an interrogative term *(comment, où, pourquoi, quand, qui)* followed by *ça.*

Examples:

Y schlingue, lui!
(who) ***Qui ça?***

J'pars maintenant.
(why) ***Pourquoi ça?***

1. La nana, è s'fait d'la bile.
   (why) ________________ ?
2. On s'est bien marré!
   (where) ________________ ?
3. J'vais la brancher maintenant.
   (how) ________________ ?
4. J'vais pas boire d'alcool. J'vais grenouiller, c'est tout.
   (why) ________________ ?
5. Y fume ses clopes l'une après l'autre.
   (who) ________________ ?
6. Tu veux m'accompagner, mon vieux?
   (where) ________________ ?
7. J'ai la trouille.
   (why) ________________ ?
8. J'en pince pour elle.
   (whom) ________________ ?
9. J'me fringue toujours bien l'soir.
   (why) ________________ ?
10. Marie, l'était ronde comme une queue d'billard.
    (when) ________________ ?

DICTATION

Test Your Aural Comprehension.

(This dictation can be found in Appendix A on page 238)

If you are following along with your cassette, you will now hear a paragraph containing many of the terms from this section. The paragraph will be read at normal conversational speed (which may actually seem fast to you at first). In addition, the words will be pronounced as you would actually hear them in a conversation, including many common reductions.

The first time the paragraph is presented, simply listen in order to get accustomed to the speed and heavy use of reductions. The paragraph will then be read again with a pause after each group of words to give you time to write down what you heard. The third time the paragraph is read, follow along with what you have written.

REVIEW EXAM FOR LESSONS 1-5

(Answers to Review, p. 224)

A. Underline the word(s) that fall into the same category as the words to the left.

1. **eat**: a. se goinfrer b. tomber des cordes c. bouffer d. se taper la cloche

2. **drunk**: a. poivrot b. nana c. rond comme une queue de billard d. bourré

3. **rain**: a. filer b. tomber des cordes c. saucée d. flotter

4. **look**: a. mater b. zieuter c. bigler d. brancher

5. **family**: a. boui-boui b. frangin c. fric d. frangine

6. **leave**: a. planquer b. encarrer c. se carapater d. se tirer

7. **fight**: a. s'engueuler b. se bouffer le nez c. bagarre d. boum

8. **to drink**: a. s'en jeter un derrière la cravate b. s'humecter les amygdales c. schlinguer d. picoler

9. **food**: a. faire un gueuleton b. bouffe c. boustifaille d. coin

10. **to arrive**: a. piquer b. se pointer c. cailler d. radiner

11. **alcohol**: a. tord-boyaux b. nickel c. frangin d. brouille-ménage

12. **money**: a. schlingue b. pognon c. fric d. balle

B. Complete the following phrases by choosing the appropriate word(s) from the list below. Give the correct form of the verb.

baraque	**filer**	**nana**
cailler	**marrant**	**pommes**
clope	**mauvais poil**	**schlinguer**
dingue	**moutards**	**trouille**

1. Quelle odeur affreuse! Qu'est-c'que ça ________________ ici!
2. J'ai envie d'fumer. Passe-moi une ______________ .
3. Regarde c'type-là. Y parle tout seul! J'crois qu'il est ____________ !
4. L'est jolie, c'te __________ .
5. Y fait froid aujourd'hui. J'commence à ________________ .
6. Les ________________ de ma voisine, y font trop d'bruit.
7. Daniel, y m'fait toujours rire. Qu'est-c'qu'y peut êt' ____________ !
8. J'suis toujours de ________________ avant d'prend'mon café.
9. Tu habites depuis longtemps dans c'te ______________ ?
10. J'ai le vertige, moi. J'crois qu'jvais tomber dans les ____________ !
11. Quand j'ai vu l'voleur, j'ai eu la ______________ !
12. Tu m'dois du fric! ______________-moi mille balles tout d'suite!

C. CROSSWORD PUZZLE

Complete the sentences by using the list below. Write your answer in the crossword puzzle on the opposite page.

balles	**bousiller**	**cramer**
bordel	**chiales**	**fringuée**
boudin	**claquer**	**pébroc**
boule	**cradingue**	**pince**

ACROSS

7. C't'un fou! Il a perdu la ______ !

18. J'ai pas d'fric sur moi. Tu peux m'prêter cent ______ ?

23. J'viens d'______ tout mon fric!

29. Quelle jolie robe! T'es bien ______ ce soir.

34. Pourquoi tu ______ ? T'es pas content?

41. J'veux pas bouffer dans c'resto. L'est ______ !

DOWN

7. Quel ______ ta chambre! Va la ranger tout d'suite!

12. Y flotte! J'dois chercher mon ______ .

18. Attention! Tu vas ______ c'guindal!

36. Y flotte! Encore un pique-nique qui est allé en eau d'______ .

39. L'est belle, c'te nana. J'en ______ pour elle.

41. Y fait chaud aujourd'hui. J'commence à ______ .

CROSSWORD PUZZLE

D. CONTEXT EXERCISE
Fill in the letter corresponding to the correct phrase in the right column.

☐ 1. Marcel, l'est marié?

☐ 2. J'vais à Paris ce soir. Je s'rai treize heures dans l'avion.

☐ 3. Tu la connais bien?

☐ 4. Suzanne, l'a fait quoi quand l'médecin, y lui a dit qu'elle était enceinte?

☐ 5. Tu peux pas entrer dans l'resto comme ça,

☐ 6. T'es malade?

☐ 7. C'est ton meilleur ami?

☐ 8. Tu veux faire un pique-nique ici?

☐ 9. Où tu vas?

☐ 10. Quelqu'un a encore volé mon vélo!

☐ 11. Tu veux aller au ciné?

☐ 12. Y commence à pleuvoir.

A. Tu **rigoles**! J'savais pas qu'c'était aussi loin qu'ça!

B. D'accord. C'est tranquille comme **coin**.

C. J'vais **m'balader** un peu. Je r'viens bientôt.

D. T'es trop **mal fringué**.

E. Mais non! J'l'aime pas du tout, c'**mec**-là!

F. J'**en ai marre**! C'est la troisième fois qu'ça m'arrive en un mois! J'appelle la police!

G. Oui. J'crois que j'vais rester au **plumard**.

H. J'vais chercher mon **pébroc**.

I. J'peux pas. J'ai pas assez d'**fric**.

J. L'est **tombée dans les pommes**.

K. Non, j'l'ai **branchée** pour la première fois c't'après-midi.

L. Mais, oui! L'a **signé un bail** la semaine dernière.

Le *Chouchou* du Prof

*(The teacher's **pet**)*

(En Classe)

Leçon Six

Dialogue in slang

Le Chouchou du Prof

André: Oh, **la vache**! Le **paquet** de devoirs qu'il **fiche** aux **potaches**, ce **prof**... ce n'est pas croyable!

Yvette: Je n'ai même pas le temps de les faire parce que je dois **bosser** ce soir. Je crois que je vais **sécher le cours** demain.

André: Mais tu t'es **fait étendre** au dernier **exam**, toi et il y en a un autre vendredi.

Yvette: Je sais bien. Et si je ne le **potasse** pas, je suis **frite**!

André: Il doit être **cinglé** de penser qu'on peut lire tous ces **bouquins** en deux jours! Je crois qu'il est **sado**.

Yvette: Ben, oui! Sachant que je ne suis pas **calée** en **maths**, il me pose toujours des **colles** et me fait **plancher** devant toute la **galerie**. Il me **casse les pieds**, lui!

André: Mais tu as remarqué que son **chouchou** semble toujours **cartonner** aux examens? Il ne reçoit que des **méganotes**!

Yvette: Je ne peux pas le **blairer**, ce **gonze**! En plus, il est **moche à caler des roues de corbillard**. Et il **a un œil qui dit zut à l'autre**!

André: Et tu as **zieuté** un peu ses **tifs**? A chaque fois qu'il **se fait déboiser la colline**, le **merlan** fait de sa tête un **melon déplumé**.

Lesson Six

Translation in English

André: **Holy cow**! The **stack** of homework the **teacher piles** on **students** is unreal!

Yvette: I don't even have time to do it because I have **to work** tonight. I think I'll **cut class** tomorrow.

André: But you **flunked** the last **exam** and there's another one on Friday.

Yvette: I know. And if I don't **cram for it**, I'm **done for**!

André: He must be **out of his mind** to think that we can read all these **books** in two days! I think he's a **sadist**.

Yvette: I'll say! Knowing that I'm **lousy** in **math**, he always puts these **impossible questions** to me and **grills me** in front of the entire **class**. He **ticks me off**!

André: But did you notice that his **pet** always seems **to ace** the exams? All he ever does is get **high grades**!

Yvette: I can't **stand** that **guy**! Besides, he's **got a face that could stop the wheels of a hearse**. And he's really **cross-eyed**!

André: And did you **get a load of** his **hair**? Every time he **gets his hair cut** the **barber** makes him look like a **plucked melon**.

Leçon Six

Dialogue in slang as it would be spoken

Le Chouchou du Prof

André: Oh, **la vache**! Le **paquet** d'devoirs qu'y **fiche** aux **potaches**, ce **prof**... c'est pas croyable!

Yvette: J'ai même pas l'temps d'les faire pasque j'dois **bosser** c'soir. J'crois que j'vais **sécher l'cours** demain.

André: Mais tu t'es **fait étendre** au dernier **exam**, toi et y en a un aut'vendredi.

Yvette: J'sais bien. Et si j'le **potasse** pas, j'suis **frite**!

André: Y doit êt'**cinglé** d'penser qu'on peut lire tous ces **bouquins** en deux jours! J'crois qu'il est **sado**.

Yvette: Ben, oui! Sachant que j'suis pas **calée** en **maths**, y m'pose toujours des **colles** et m'fait **plancher** d'vant toute la **galerie**. Y m'**casse les pieds**, lui!

André: Mais t'as r'marqué qu'son **chouchou**, y semb' toujours **cartonner** aux exams? Y r'çoit qu'des **méganotes**!

Yvette: J'peux pas l'**blairer**, c'**gonze**! En plus, l'est **moche à caler des roues d'corbillard**. Et l'**a un œil qui dit zut à l'autre**!

André: Et t'as **zieuté** un peu ses **tifs**? A chaque fois qu'y **s'fait déboiser la colline**, le **merlan**, y fait d'sa tête un **melon déplumé**.

Vocabulary

blairer quelqu'un (ne pas pouvoir) *v.* to be unable to stand or tolerate someone.

example: Je ne peux pas le **blairer**!

as spoken: J'peux pas l'**blairer**!

translation: I can't **stand** him!

NOTE (1): **blair** *n.* nose, "schnoz," "honker."

example: Jimmy Durante était connu pour son grand **blair**.

as spoken: Jimmy Durante, l'était connu pour son grand **blair**.

translation: Jimmy Durante was known for his big **honker**.

NOTE (2): **ne pas pouvoir blairer quelqu'un** could be loosely translated as "to be unable to tolerate someone to the point that even smelling him would be too much to bear."

SYNONYM: **pif** *m.*

bosser *v.* to work hard.

example: Je suis fatigué parce que je **bosse** soixante heures par semaine.

as spoken: J'suis fatigué pasque j'**bosse** soixante heures par s'maine.

translation: I'm tired because I **work** sixty hours a week.

SYNONYM (1): **boulonner** *v.* to work hard • (lit); to tighten bolts.

SYNONYM (2): **boulotter** *v.* to work • **boulot** *n.* work, job.

bouquin *m.* book.

example: Tu as lu tout ce **bouquin** en une heure?

as spoken: T'as lu tout c'**bouquin** en une heure?

translation: You read that entire **book** in one hour?

NOTE (1): The word **bouquin** from the Dutch word for "small book," has now become a popular slang synonym for "book" in general.

NOTE (2): **bouquiner** *v.* to read • (lit); to go through books.

calé(e) en quelque chose (être) *adj.* to be very smart in a particular subject, to be an expert • (lit); to be wedged, securely installed in something.

example: J'ai toujours une calculatrice dans mon sac. Je ne suis pas du tout **calée** en maths!

as spoken: J'ai toujours une calculatrice dans mon sac. J'suis pas du tout **calée** en maths!

translation: I always have a calculator in my purse. I'm not at all **smart** when it comes to math!

SYNONYM: **fortiche en quelque chose (être)** *exp.* • (lit); strong, a slang deformation of the adjective *fort(e)* meaning "strong."

cartonner à un examen *v.* to ace a test.

example: J'ai **cartonné** à l'examen!

as spoken: [no change]

translation: I **aced** the test!

NOTE: The verb **cartonner** literally means " to hit a target." It refers to the cardboard target, or **carton**, that is found in shooting ranges or amusement parks.

casser les pieds à quelqu'un *exp.* to annoy someone greatly • (lit); to break someone's feet.

example: Tu me **casses les pieds** avec toutes tes questions!

as spoken: Tu m'**casses les pieds** avec toutes tes questions!

translation: You really **annoy** me with all your questions!

VARIATION: **Tu me les casses!** • You're breaking them!

NOTE: **casse-pieds** *m.&f.* annoying person, pain in the neck.

SYNONYM: **taper sur le système à quelqu'un** *exp.* to get on someone's nerves • (lit); to hit on someone's system.

chouchou(te) *n.* teacher's pet.

example: David est le **chouchou** du professeur. C'est pour ça qu'il reçoit toujours de bonnes notes!

as spoken: David, c'est l'**chouchou** du prof~. C'est pour ça qu'y r'çoit toujours de bonnes notes!

translation: David is the teacher's **pet**. That's why he always gets good grades!

NOTE (1): **chouchouter** *v.* to spoil (someone).

NOTE (2): It is common to hear *mon chou* or *mon chouchou* used as a term of endearment. Contrary to what one might think, *mon chou* does not mean "my cabbage," but rather "my cream puff" as in the popular French pastry *chou à la crème.*

cinglé(e) (être) *adj.* to be crazy, nuts.

example: J'ai entendu dire que tu comptes sauter en parachute demain! Mais, tu es **cinglé**, non?

as spoken: J'ai entendu dire que tu comptes sauter en parachute demain! Mais, t'es **cinglé**, non?

translation: I heard that you're planning on going parachuting tomorrow! Are you **nuts**?

SYNONYM (1): **dingue (être)** *adj.*

SYNONYM (2): **déménager** *v.* to go crazy • (lit); to move (out of one's mind).

colle *f.* a difficult question to answer, "a sticky question" • (lit); glue.

example: La prof m'a posé une **colle**!

as spoken: La prof, è m'a posé une **colle**!

translation: The teacher asked me a **sticky question**!

ALSO: **coller un étudiant** *exp.* to flunk a student.

déboiser la colline (se faire) *exp.* to get a haircut • (lit); to deforest or untimber one's hill.

example: Je vois que tu **t'es fait déboiser la colline**! Ça te va très bien!

as spoken: J'vois qu'tu **t'es fait déboiser la colline**! Ça t'va très bien!

translation: I see you **got a haircut**! It looks really good on you!

étendre (se faire) *exp.* to flunk, to blow a test • (lit); to get oneself stretched out.

example: Je **me suis fait étendre** à mon examen!

as spoken: Je **m'suis fait étendre** à mon exam~!

translation: My test went badly. I **totally blew it**!

SYNONYM: **coller (se faire)** *v.*

exam *m.* a popular abbreviation of "*examen*" meaning "test."

example: La semaine prochaine, ma frangine va passer son **exam** de psychologie. Elle a la trouille!

as spoken: La s'maine prochaine, ma frangine, è va passer son **exam** de psycho. L'a la trouille!

translation: Next week, my sister is going to take her psychology **test**. She's scared to death!

fiche (a variation of *ficher*) *v.* **1.** to give • **2.** to put • **3.** to do.

example (1): **Fiche**-moi ça!

as spoken: [no change]

translation: **Give** me that!

example (2): **Fiche**-le sur la table.

as spoken: [no change]

translation: Put it on the table.

example (3): Tu **fiches** quoi ici?

as spoken: [no change]

translation: What are you **doing** here?

NOTE (1): Oddly enough, **fiche** is a verb (although it does not have a traditional ending) and is conjugated as a regular "er" verb: *je fiche, tu fiches, il/elle fiche, nous fichons, vous fichez, ils fichent*. However, its past participle is that of a regular "re" verb: *fichu(e)*.

NOTE (2): The stronger form of the verb **fiche** is **foutre**: *See NOTE (2), p. .48*

frit(e) (être) *adj*. to be done for • (lit); to be fried.

example: Si le patron me trouve ici, je suis **frit**!

as spoken: Si l'patron m'trouve ici, j'suis **frit**!

translation: If the boss finds me ici, I'm **done for**!

SYNONYM: **cuit(e) (être)** *adj*. • (lit); to be cooked.

galerie *f*. public (in general).

example: Tu m'as embarrassé devant toute la **galerie**!

as spoken: Tu m'as embarrassé d'vant toute la **gal'rie**!

translation: You embarrassed me in front of **everyone**!

gonze *m*. guy, "dude."

example: Tu connais ce **gonze**-là? C'est mon nouveau professeur.

as spoken: Tu connais c'**gonze**-là? C'est mon nouveau prof~.

translation: Do you know this **guy**? He's my new teacher.

NOTE: **gonzesse** *f*. girl, "chick."

SYNONYM (1): **mec** *m. (extremely popular), p. 52.*

SYNONYM (2): **zigue** *m.*

"La vache!" *exclam.* "Wow!" • (lit); the cow.

example: Oh, **la vache**! Tu as vu ça?

as spoken: Oh, **la vache**! T'as vu ça?

translation: **Wow**! Did you see that?

NOTE: **"La vache!"** has nothing to do with "cow" although this is the literal translation. It is used in much the same way as the English expression, "Holy cow!"

ALSO (1): **vache** *adj.* mean,tough.

example: Mon nouveau prof d'anglais est très **vache** avec les étudiants.

as spoken: Mon nouveau prof d'anglais, l'est très **vache** avec les étudiants.

translation: My new English teacher is very **mean** with the students.

ALSO (2): **vacherie** *f.* mean, rotten trick.

maths *m.pl.* abbreviation of "mathematics."

example: Je suis nul en **maths**.

as spoken: J'suis nul en **maths**.

translation: I'm a big zero when it comes to **math**.

NOTE: In colloquial French, many academic subjects may be abbreviated such as **bio** *f.* biology; **géo** *f.* geography; **gym** *f.* gymnastics; **philo** *f.* philosophy, **psycho** *f.* psychology.

méganote *f.* a high grade • (lit); a mega-grade.

example: J'ai eu une **méganote** à mon examen de géographie!

as spoken: J'ai eu une **méganote** à mon exam~ de géo~!

translation: I got a **really high grade** on my geography test!

NOTE: In the above, the prepositon *à* and not *sur* followed the noun *méganote*, a common mistake made by native English speakers.

melon déplumé (avoir le) *exp.* (humorous) to be completely bald • (lit); to have a plucked melon (for a head).

example: Un de ces jours, tu auras **le melon déplumé** comme ton vieux.

as spoken: Un d'ces jours, t'auras **l'melon déplumé** comme ton vieux.

translation: One of these days, you'll be **bald** just like your ol' man.

merlan *m.* barber • (lit); whiting (fish).

example: Je vais aller chez le **merlan** me faire couper les cheveux.

as spoken: J'vais aller chez l'**merlan** m'faire couper les ch'veux.

translation: I'm going to go to the **barber** to get my hair cut.

moche à caler des roues de corbillard (être) *exp.* (humorous) to be extremely ugly • (lit); to be ugly enough to stop the wheels of a hearse.

example: Il est **moche à caler des roues de corbillard**, lui!

as spoken: L'est **moche à caler des roues d'corbillard**, lui!

translation: He has **a face that could stop a clock**.

SYNONYM (1): **naze (être)** *adj. (extremely popular).*

SYNONYM (2): **laid(e) à faire peur (être)** *exp.* • (lit); to be ugly enough to cause fear.

ALSO: **moche** *adj.* ugly, nasty, unpleasant, mean.

example: Pourquoi tu lui as parlé si brusquement? C'est vraiment **moche** de ta part.

as spoken: [no change]

translation: Why were you so rough talking to him? It was really **mean** of you.

SYNONYM: **dégueulasse/dégueu** *adj.*

paquet *m.* a lot, "a pile" • (lit); a package.

example: J'ai un **paquet** de soucis aujourd'hui!

as spoken: J'ai un **paquet** d'soucis aujourd'hui!

translation: I have a **pile** of worries today!

ALSO: **mettre le paquet** *exp.* to do something with abandon, to let out all the stops.

example: J'ai invité des amis à dîner; j'ai fait la cuisine toute la journée. J'ai vraiment **mis le paquet**.

as spoken: J'ai invité des amis à dîner; j'ai fait la cuisine toute la journée. J'ai vraiment **mis l'paquet**.

translation: I invited some friends for dinner; I cooked all day. I really **let out all the stops**.

plancher *v.* to be interrogated by a teacher.

example: Chaque fois que le prof me fait **plancher**, je deviens super nerveux.

as spoken: Chaque fois que l'prof, y m'fait **plancher**, je d'viens super nerveux.

translation: Every time the teacher **grills** me, I get super nervous.

NOTE: This comes from the word "*planche*" (meaning "board") and carries with it an implication of stiffness due to fear.

potache *m.* student.

example: Quand j'étais **potache**, je n'avais jamais le temps de me marrer.

as spoken: Quand j'étais **potache**, j'avais jamais l'temps de m'marrer.

translation: When I was a **student**, I never had time to have any fun.

potasser *v.* to study hard, to bone up on (a subject).

example: Je dois **potasser** mon français ce soir.

as spoken: J'dois **potasser** mon français c'soir.

translation: I have **to bone up on** my French tonight.

prof *m. & f.* teacher, professor.

example: Tu as vu la nouvelle **prof** d'anglais? Elle est très jeune, elle!

as spoken: T'as vu la nouvelle **prof** d'anglais? L'est très jeune, elle!

translation: Did you see the new English **teacher**? She's so young!

NOTE: The word **professeur** is a masculine noun. However, its abbreviated form, **prof** is both masculine *and* feminine.

sado (être) *n. & adj.* a common abbreviation of *sadique* meaning "sadist" or "sadistic."

example: Je n'aime pas aller chez mon dentiste. Je crois qu'il est **sado**!

as spoken: J'aime pas allez chez mon dentiste. J'crois qu'il est **sado**!

translation: I don't like going to my dentist. I think he's a **sadist**!

sécher *v.* to cut class • (lit); to dry.

example: J'ai **séché** mon cours de biologie aujourd'hui pour aller au cinéma.

as spoken: J'ai **séché** mon cours de bio~ aujourd'hui pour aller au cinoche.

translation: I **skipped** my biology class today in order to go to the movies.

NOTE: **cinoche** *m.* a popular slang form of *cinéma.*

tifs *m.pl.* hair.

example: Ma frangine a des **tifs** très longs. Ils descendent jusqu'à ses genoux!

as spoken: Ma frangine, l'a des **tifs** très longs. Y descendent jusqu'à ses genoux!

translation: My sister has very long **hair**. It goes down to her knees!

un œil qui dit zut à l'autre (avoir) *exp.* (humorous) said of someone who is cross-eyed • (lit); to have an eye which says "Darn!" to the other.

example: Quand elle me regarde, avec son **œil qui dit zut à l'autre**, j'ai le tournis!

as spoken: Quand è m'regarde, avec son **œil qui dit zut à l'autre**, j'ai l'tournis!

translation: When she looks at me with her **crossed eyes**, I get dizzy.

NOTE: **avoir le tournis** *exp.* to have dizziness.

SYNONYM: **un œil qui joue au billard et l'autre qui compte les points (avoir)** *exp.* • (lit); to have one eye that's playing billiards while the other is off counting the points.

zieuter *v.* to look • (lit); to eye.

example: Tu as **zieuté** l'arc-en-ciel? C'était incroyable!

as spoken: T'as **zieuté** l'arc-en-ciel? C'était incroyable!

translation: Did you look at the rainbow? It was unbelievable!

NOTE (1): This comes from *les yeux* (pronounced: *les z'yeux* • *z'yeux* = **zyeuter**).

NOTE (2): Also spelled **zyeuter**.

Practice The Vocabulary 

(Answers to Lesson 6, p. 225)

A. Complete the phrases by choosing the appropriate word(s) from the list. Give the correct form of the verb.

blairer	**casser**	**merlan**
bosser	**déboiser**	**moche**
bouquin	**étendre**	**tifs**
calé	**la vache**	**zieuter**

1. J'peux pas aller danser pasque j'dois ____________ ce soir.

2. L'est pas populaire, c'prof. Personne peut le ____________ .

3. J'peux rien ______________ sans lunettes.

4. J'ai lu tout un ______________ en deux heures.

5. Mais arrête de m' ______________ les pieds!

6. Oh, ________________ ! L'est belle, c'te nana!

7. Michel, l'est ______________ à caler des roues de corbillard.

8. Un savant, ça doit être ______________ en maths.

9. Tu t'es fait ________________ à l'examen?

10. Y sont longs tes ____________ . Pourquoi tu vas pas chez l' ________________ pour t'faire _________________ la colline?

B. Underline the word in parentheses that best completes the phrase.

1. T'as claqué tout ton fric? T'es (**cinglé**, **lessivé**, **peinard**), non?

2. J'dois (**piquer**, **potasser**, **gueuletonner**) c't'exam pasque j'veux pas m'faire (**ligoter**, **draguer**, **étendre**).

3. Pour mon cours de bio, j'ai une très bonne (**idée**, **prof**, **promenade**). L'est très jeune d'ailleurs!

4. Y s'est fait (**déguiser**, **déboiser**, **délayer**) la colline et maintenant l'a l'(**fruit**, **abricot**, **melon**) déplumé.

5. Y nous (**fiche**, **pique**, **cuisine**) toujours un (**fiston**, **fromage**, **paquet**) d'devoirs.

6. Le prof, y m'a fait (**draguer**, **plancher**, **casser**) d'vant toute la (**voiture**, **baraque**, **galerie**).

7. C'est l'(**chouchou**, **chat**, **charbon**) du prof.

8. Y a une trentaine de (**pots**, **porcs**, **potaches**) dans mon cours d'musique.

9. Ma sœur, l'est pas (**au courant**, **calée**, **amusante**) en (**livres**, **maths**, **bouffe**).

10. Alors, l'exam, y s'est bien passé? Oui! J'ai r'çu une (**notation**, **mininote**, **méganote**)!

11. J'l'ai pas vu en classe aujourd'hui. Il a (**mouillé**, **séché**, **nettoyé**) l'cours.

C. Underline the synonym.

1. **blairer:** a. sentir b. courir c. sourire
2. **moche:** a. gentil b. amusant c. laid
3. **cinglé:** a. fou b. intelligent c. malade
4. **calé:** a. riche b. expert c. idiot
5. **bouquin:** a. porte b. maison c. livre
6. **bosser:** a. parler b. travailler c. donner
7. **fiche:** a. courir b. donner c. s'évanouir
8. **paquet:** a. beaucoup de b. peu de c. grand
9. **potasser:** a. partir b. se fâcher c. étudier
10. **zieuter:** a. regarder b. tomber c. travailler
11. **gonze:** a. restaurant b. individu c. clé
12. **cartonner:** a. marcher b. dormir c. réussir

A CLOSER LOOK:

Colloquial Use of Present Tense to Indicate Future

In colloquial French, the present tense is commonly used to indicate an event that will take place in the future. It is important to note that this construction is used by all social levels. For example:

On en parle plus tard.
We'll talk about it later.

Je r'viens dans une heure.
I'll be back in an hour.

J'le fais d'main.
I'll do it tomorrow.

This also holds true when using "if" and "then" clauses. Ordinarily, when the "if" clause is in the present tense, the "then" clause is in the future tense:

Si tu m'rends c'service, J'te donn'rai mon nouveau disque.
If you do me this favor, I **will** give you my new record.

Si tu viens chez moi, j'te f'rai un bon dîner.
If you come to my house, I **will** make you a good dinner.

S'y m'pose encore des questions, j'répondrai pas.
If he asks me more questions, I **will** not answer.

However, using the colloquial construction, the "then" clause remains in the present tense even though a reference to an event taking place in the future is being made.

Si tu m'rends c'service, j'te donne mon nouveau disque.
If you do me this favor, I **will** give you my new record.

Si tu viens chez moi, j'te fais un bon dîner.
If you come to my house, I **will** make you a good dinner.

S'y m'pose encore des questions, j'réponds pas.
If he asks me more questions, I **will** not answer.

EXERCISES

A. Rewrite the phrases by implementing the colloquial use of the present tense to indicate future.

1. On s'verra d'main, alors?
   (We'll see each other tomorrow then?)

   ____

2. J'te l'donn'rai après l'déjeuner
   (I'll give it to you after lunch.)

   ____

3. On l'f'ra plus tard
   (We'll do it later.)

   ____

4. On en discut'ra d'main.
   (We'll discuss it tomorrow.)

   ____

5. J'te la présent'rai à la soirée.
   (I'll introduce you to her at the party.)

   ____

6. Y te l'rendra c'soir.
   (He'll give it back to you tonight.)

   ____

7. J'viendrai t'chercher à 8h.
   (I'll come by to pick you up at 8:00.)

   ____

8. Ce soir, è lui f'ra une grande surprise!
   (Tonight, she's going to give him a big surpise.)

   ____

9. C't'après-midi, on fêt'ra ton anniversaire.
   (This afternoon, we're going to celebrate your birthday.)

   ____

10. J'te pass'rai un coup d'fil demain.
    (I'll give you a telephone call tomorrow.)

    ____

DICTATION
Test Your Aural Comprehension.

(This dictation can be found in Appendix A on page 239)

If you are following along with your cassette, you will now hear a paragraph containing many of the terms from this section. The paragraph will be read at normal conversational speed (which may actually seem fast to you at first). In addition, the words will be pronounced as you would actually hear them in a conversation, including many common reductions.

The first time the paragraph is presented, simply listen in order to get accustomed to the speed and heavy use of reductions. The paragraph will then be read again with a pause after each group of words to give you time to write down what you heard. The third time the paragraph is read, follow along with what you have written.

La Vie de *Cossard*

(The life of a **lazy bum***)*

(Les Vacances)

Leçon Sept

Dialogue in slang

La Vie de Cossard

Yves: Salut, Marc! Tu as passé de bonnes vacances?

Marc: Elles étaient **sensass**! J'aurai du mal à **reprendre le collier**, crois-moi. J'ai **enfilé des perles** pendant un mois en vrai **cossard**.

Yves: **Moi itou**. Quand je suis en vacances, je n'**en fiche pas une rame** et franchement, je préfère les passer tout seul! Une fois, j'ai pris mes vacances avec mon frangin et au bout de trois jours, il a commencé à me **taper sur les nerfs**. Moi, je préfère passer mon temps à **lézarder** tandis que lui, il a toujours la **bougeotte**. Et qu'est-ce qu'il peut être **collant**!

Marc: Tu aurais dû essayer de le **semer**.

Yves: Eh ben, pour qu'il **s'éclipse** quelques **plombes**, je lui **balançais** du **pognon** pour le **cinoche.** C'était du **gâteau**!

Marc: **Chapeau**! Faut dire que tu es **roublard**, toi.

Yves: Bon, **revenons à nos moutons**...tu as **pioncé à la belle étoile** comme tu voulais?

Marc: Non, on a décidé de **descendre** dans un hôtel à pension complète. J'avais la **crèche**, la **dîne** et tout.

Yves: J'espère que tu ne t'es pas fait **arnaquer**. Moi, je suis toujours **fauché** après être descendu dans un bon hôtel avec les notes **salées** qu'ils te balancent.

Marc: Tu vas **en rester baba** quand je te dirai le prix. Ça ne m'a pas coûté une **thune** vu que mon père est le **proprio**!

Lesson Seven

Translation in English

Yves: Hi, Marc! Did you have a good vacation?

Marc: It was **sensational**! I'm gonna have trouble **getting back to the grind**, believe me. I just **hung out and did nothing** for a month like a real **lazy slob**!

Yves: **The same goes for me**. When I'm on vacation, I **don't lift a finger**, and frankly, I prefer to go alone! Once I went on vacation with my brother and by the end of three days, he started **getting on my nerves**. I prefer spending my time **soaking up the rays** whereas he always has to be **on the move**. And can he ever be **clingy**!

Marc: You should've tried **to ditch him**.

Yves: Well, just so he'd **get lost** for a couple of **hours**, I **would hand him** some **cash** for the **movies.** It was **a cinch**!

Marc: **Bravo**! I must say you're really **sneaky**.

Yves: Okay, **getting back to what we were talking about**...did you **sleep under the stars** like you wanted?

Marc: No, we decided **to check into** a hotel with everything included. I had **room**, **board**, and everything.

Yves: I hope you didn't get **ripped off**. I'm always **broke** after staying in a nice hotel with the **inflated** bills they throw at you.

Marc: You're going **to be shocked** when I tell you the price. It didn't cost me a **red cent** because my father is the **owner**!

Leçon Sept

Dialogue in slang as it would be spoken

La Vie d'Cossard

Yves: Salut, Marc! T'as passé d'bonnes vacances?

Marc: Z'étaient **sensass**! J'aurai du mal à **reprend'le collier**, crois-moi. J'ai **enfilé des perles** pendant un mois en vrai **cossard**.

Yves: **Moi itou**. Quand j'suis en vacances, j'**en fiche pas une rame** et franchement, j'préfère les passer tout seul! Une fois, j'ai pris mes vacances avec mon frangin et au bout de trois jours, l'a commencé à m'**taper sur les nerfs**. Moi, j'préfère passer mon temps à **lézarder** tandis que lui, l'a toujours la **bougeotte**. Et qu'est-c'qu'y peut êt'**collant**!

Marc: T'aurais dû essayer de l'**semer**.

Yves: Eh ben, pour qu'y **s'éclipse** quèques **plombes**, j'lui **balançais** du **pognon** pour le **cinoche**. C'était du **gâteau**!

Marc: **Chapeau**! Faut dire que t'es **roublard**, toi.

Yves: Bon, **rev'nons à nos moutons**...t'as **pioncé à la belle étoile** comme tu voulais?

Marc: Non, on a décidé d'**descend'** dans un hôtel à pension complète. J'avais la **crèche**, la **dîne** et tout.

Yves: J'espère que tu t'es pas fait **arnaquer**. Moi, j'suis toujours **fauché** après êt'descendu dans un bon hôtel avec les notes **salées** qu'y t'balancent.

Marc: Tu vas **en rester baba** quand j'te dirai l'prix. Ça m'a pas coûté une **thune** vu qu'mon père, c'est l'**proprio**!

Vocabulary

arnaquer *v.* to rip off, cheat someone • (lit); to sting.

example: Je viens d'acheter une nouvelle montre, mais elle ne marche pas! Cette vendeuse, elle m'a **arnaqué**!

as spoken: J'viens d'acheter une nouvelle montre, mais è marche pas! Cette vendeuse, è m'a **arnaqué**!

translation: I just bought a new watch, but it's not working! That saleswoman **ripped me off**!

ALSO: **se faire arnaquer** *exp.* to get oneself ripped off.

example: Tu as payé combien? Je crois que tu t'es fait **arnaquer** chez le mécanicien.

as spoken: T'as payé combien? J'crois qu'tu t'es fait **arnaquer** chez l'mécano.

translation: You paid how much? I think you got **ripped off** at the mechanic's.

NOTE: In France, the movie classic *The Hustler*, starring Paul Newman, is known as *L'Arnaqueur* and the popular Newman-Redford comedy, *The Sting*, is called *L'Arnaque*.

SYNONYM: **avoir (se faire)** *exp.*

example: J'ai payé 50 dollars un pullover qui en vaut 20. Je **me suis fait avoir**!

as spoken: J'ai payé 50 dollars un pull~ qui en vaut 20. Je **m'suis fait avoir**!

translation: I paid 50 dollars for a pullover that was worth 20. I **got ripped off**!

ALSO: *On m'a* ***eu****!* = I was had!

balancer *v.* to throw • (lit); to balance.

example: Le chien a bousillé ma montre! Quand je le trouverai, je vais le **balancer** dehors!

as spoken: Le chien, l'a bousillé ma montre! Quand j'le trouv'rai, j'vais l'**balancer** dehors!

translation: The dog broke my watch! When I find him, I'm gonna **throw** him outside!

ALSO: **s'en balancer** *v.* not to care.

example: La politique, je **m'en balance**!

as spoken: La politique, j'**m'en balance**!

translation: I **don't give a hoot** about politics!

bougeotte (avoir la) *exp.* to have the fidgets, to have ants in one's pants.

example: Tu ne peux pas rester tranquille cinq minutes?! Qu'est-ce que tu as la **bougeotte**, toi!

as spoken: Tu ~ peux pas rester tranquille cinq minutes?! Qu'est-c'que t'as la **bougeotte**, toi!

translation: You can't sit still for five minutes?! Are you ever **fidgety**!

NOTE: This expression comes from the verb *bouger* meaning "to move" or "to budge."

"Chapeau!" *exclam.* "Bravo!" "Hats off!" • (lit); "Hat!"

example: J'ai entendu dire que tu es devenu papa! **Chapeau**!

as spoken: J'ai entendu dire qu' t'es dev'nu dab! **Chapeau**!

translation: I heard that you became a father! **Congratulations**!

NOTE (1): This is an abbreviation of: *Je vous tire mon chapeau!;* I tip my hat to you!

NOTE (2): The expression "to hear that..." does not quite translate the same into French. The verb **dire** ("to say") must be added to **entendre** ("to hear"): **entendre dire que** *exp.* • (lit); to hear say that...!

cinoche *n.* an abbreviation of "*cinéma,*" meaning "movie theater."

example: Tu veux m'accompagner au **cinoche** ce soir?

as spoken: [no change]

translation: You wanna go to the **movies** with me tonight?

collant(e) (être) *adj.* to be clingy, said of someone who is hard to get rid of • (lit); to be sticky.

example: Il me suit partout! Qu'est-ce qu'il est **collant**!

as spoken: Y m'suit partout! Qu'est-c'qu'il est **collant**!

translation: He follows me everywhere! He's so **clingy**!

cossard *m.* a lazy individual, a lazy bum.

example: Tu ne fais rien toute la journée. Quel **cossard**!

as spoken: Tu ~ fais rien toute la journée. Quel **cossard**!

translation: You don't do a thing all day. What a **lazy bum**!

NOTE: **avoir la cosse** *exp.* to be lazy.

example: Ce n'est pas la peine de lui demander de nous aider. Il **a la cosse**, lui.

as spoken: C'est pas la peine de lui d'mander d'nous aider. L'**a la cosse**, lui.

translation: It's no use asking him to help us. The guy's **totally lazy**.

SYNONYM (1): **flemmard** *m.*

NOTE: **flemme (avoir la)** *exp.* to be lazy.

SYNONYM (2): **poil dans la main (avoir un)** *exp.* to be extremely lazy • (lit); to have a hair grow in one's hand, for lack of using it.

crèche *f.* room or bedroom • (lit); manger, crib.

example: Elle est petite, ta **crèche**!

as spoken: L'est p'tite, ta **crèche**!

translation: Your **bedroom** is small!

NOTE: **crécher** *v.* to live, to stay.

example: Ça fait dix ans que je **crèche** ici.

as spoken: Ça fait dix ans que j'**crèche** ici.

translation: I've **lived** here for ten years.

descendre *c.l.* a common way of saying "to stay" or "to stop in on."

example: On va **descendre** chez des amis ce soir.

as spoken: On va **descend'** chez des amis ce soir.

translation: We're going **to stay with** some friends.

NOTE: It is a common mistake among native speakers of English to say "***rester*** *dans un hôtel, chez des cousins, etc.*" since the French use the verb **descendre**.

dîne *f.* dinner.

example: C'est à quelle heure, la **dîne**?

as spoken: C't'à quelle heure, la **dîne**?

translation: What time is **dinner**?

éclipser (s') *v.* to leave quickly, to vanish • (lit); to eclipse oneself.

example: Je **me suis éclipsé** avant la conférence.

as spoken: Je **m'suis éclipsé** avant la conférence.

translation: I **snuck out** before the lecture.

NOTE: In the sentence above, the term *conférence* was translated as "lecture" not "conference." (In French, *une lecture* is "a reading.") These misinterpretations fall under the heading of *faux amis*, the many terms which appear to be similar in French and English, yet have different definitions.

enfiler des perles *exp.* to laze around and do nothing • (lit); to string pearls.

example: Je ne suis pas venu pour **enfiler des perles**! Au travail!

as spoken: J'suis pas v'nu pour **enfiler des perles**! Au boulot!

translation: I didn't come here **to just sit around**! Let's get to work!

fauché(e) (être) *adj.* to be broke • (lit); to be mowed down.

example: Je ne peux pas t'accompagner au cinoche ce soir. Je suis **fauché**.

as spoken: J'peux pas t'accompagner au cinoche ce soir. J'suis **fauché**.

translation: I can't go to the movies with you tonight. I'm **broke**.

SYNONYM: **à sec (être)** *exp.* • (lit); to be all dried up.

NOTE: The verb **faucher** (literally meaning "to mow, cut, or reap") means "to steal" in French slang. For example:

example: C'est un voleur! Il vient de **faucher** mon portefeuille!

as spoken: C't'un voleur! Y vient d'**faucher** mon portefeuille!

translation: He's a thief! He just **stole** my wallet!

SYNONYM: **piquer** *v.*

fiche une rame (ne pas en) *exp.* to do absolutely nothing • (lit); not to lift an oar.

example: Moi, je bosse toute la journée dans cette baraque et lui, il **n'en fiche pas une rame**!

as spoken: Moi, j'bosse toute la journée dans c'te baraque et lui, l'**en fiche pas une rame**!

translation: I work all day long in this house and he **doesn't lift a finger**!

gâteau (c'est du) *exp.* said of something easy, "a piece of cake" • (lit); it's cake.

example: Je vais t'apprendre à monter à vélo. **C'est du gâteau**!

as spoken: J'vais t'apprendre à monter à vélo. **C'est du gâteau**!

translation: I'm going to teach you how to ride a bike. **It's a piece of cake**!

itou *adj.* also, same.

example: Moi **itou**, j'aime le chocolat.

as spoken: Moi **itou**, j'aime le choco~.

translation: I **also** like chocolate.

lézarder *v.* (from the masculine noun *lézard* meaning "lizard") to sunbathe, to soak up the rays.

example: Je suis bronzé parce que j'ai **lézardé** toute la journée à la plage.

as spoken: J'suis bronzé pasque j'ai **lézardé** toute la journée à la plage.

translation: I'm tan because I **lied in the sun** all day at the beach.

VARIATION: **faire le lézard** exp. to sunbathe.

pioncer *v.* to sleep.

example: Je vais camper ce weekend. Ça me plaît énormément de **pioncer** à la belle étoile.

as spoken: J'vais camper c'weekend. Ça m'plaît énormément d'**pioncer** à la belle étoile.

translation: I'm going camping this weekend. I love **sleeping** under the stars.

NOTE: **à la belle étoile** *c.l.* outside • (lit); under the pretty star.

SYNONYM (1): **roupiller** *v.* • **roupillonner** *v.*

SYNONYM (2): **faire un roupillon** *exp.* to take a nap.

plombe *f.* hour.

example: Il est trois **plombes**.

as spoken: L'est trois **plombes**.

translation: It's three **o'clock**.

NOTE: This comes from the masculine noun **plomb** meaning "lead." The word **plomb** conjures up a picture of an old lead chime being struck every hour.

pognon *m.* money, "loot," "dough."

example: Tu as du **pognon** sur toi?

as spoken: T'as du **pognon** sur toi?

translation: Do you have any **money** on you?

SYNONYMS: *du fric • de l'oseille • du blé • des ronds • des sous • du pèze • des picaillons • du grisbi • de la galette*

SEE: *pognon, p. 7*

proprio *m.* an abbreviation of **propriétaire** meaning "owner" or "proprietor."

example: Je suis **proprio** d'un nouveau restaurant à Paris.

as spoken: J'suis **proprio** d'un nouveau resto à Paris.

translation: I'm the **owner** of a new restaurant in Paris.

reprendre le collier *exp.* to get back to work or school, "to get back to the grind" • (lit); to get back under the harness.

example: J'ai passé de bonnes vacances, mais demain, je dois **reprendre le collier**.

as spoken: J'ai passé d'bonnes vacances, mais d'main, j'dois **r'prend' le collier**.

translation: I had a great vacation but tomorrow I have **to get back to the grind**.

rester baba (en) *exp.* to be so stunned with amazement or surprise.

example: Richard est ton frère?! J'**en reste baba**! Je ne l'aurais jamais su si tu ne me l'avais pas dit. Vous ne vous ressemblez même pas!

as spoken: Richard, c'est ton frère?! J'**en reste baba**! J'l'aurais jamais su si tu ~ m'l'avais pas dit. Vous ~ vous r'ssemblez même pas!

translation: Richard is your brother?! I'm **stunned**! I would never have known if you hadn't told me. You don't even look alike!

"Revenons à nos moutons" *exp.* "Let's get back to what we were talking about" • (lit); "Let's get back to watching over our sheep."

example: Nous nous sommes trop écartés de notre sujet. **Revenons à nos moutons**.

as spoken: Nous nous sommes trop écartés d'not'sujet. **Rev'nons à nos moutons**.

translation: We just got way off the subject. **Let's get back to what we were talking about**.

roublard(e) (être) *adj.* to be devious or cunning.

example: Je ne me fie pas du tout à Antoine. Il est très **roublard**, celui-là.

as spoken: Je ~ m'fie pas du tout à Antoine. L'est très **roublard**, c'ui-là.

translation: I don't trust Antoine at all. He's very **devious**.

salé(e) (être) *adj.* to be expensive • (lit); to be salted.

example: Tu as claqué mille balles pour cette liquette? C'est **salé**!

as spoken: T'as claqué mille balles pour c'te liquette? C'est **salé**!

translation: You blew a thousand francs on this shirt? That's **expensive**!

NOTE: **liquette** *f.* shirt.

semer quelqu'un *v.* to ditch or shake someone • (lit); to sow someone.

example: Mon petit frangin me suit partout! Je n'arrive pas à le **semer**!

as spoken: Mon p'tit frangin, y m'suit partout! J'arrive pas à l'**semer**!

translation: My little brother follows me everywhere! I can't **ditch** him!

sensass *adj.* a common abbreviation of *sensationnel(le)* meaning "sensational."

example: Tu as vu la robe qu'elle porte, Hélène? Elle est absolument **sensass**!

as spoken: T'as vu la robe qu'è porte, Hélène? L'est absolument **sensass**!

translation: Did you see the dress Helen's wearing? It's absolutely **sensational**!

taper sur les nerfs à quelqu'un *exp.* to get on someone's nerves • (lit); to hit on someone's nerves.

example: Arrête ça tout de suite! Tu commences à **me taper sur les nerfs**, toi!

as spoken: Arrête ça tout d'suite! Tu commences à **m'taper sur les nerfs**, toi!

translation: Stop that right now! You're really starting **to get on my nerves**!

SYNONYMS: **taper/courir sur le haricot à quelqu'un** *exp.* • (lit); to hit/to run on someone's bean.

thune *f.* (also spelled *tune*) a coin.

example: Je n'en donnerais pas deux **thunes**!

as spoken: J'en donn'rais pas deux **thunes**!

translation: I wouldn't give two cents for that!

Practice The Vocabulary

(Answers to Lesson 7, p. 226)

A. Fill in the box with the letter of the appropriate fill-in.

☐ 1. J'ai enfilé des ______ tout l'après midi!
a. **diamants** b. **perles** c. **rubis**

☐ 2. Le séjour dans l'hôtel, y comprend la ______ et la ______ .
a. **entrée**, **sortie** b. **aller**, **retour** c. **crèche**, **dîne**

☐ 3. J'aime faire du camping et ______ à la belle étoile.
a. **pioncer** b. **descendre** c. **m'éclipser**

☐ 4. J'arrive pas à croire c'que tu m'dis! J'en reste ______ !
a. **baba** b. **sensass** c. **roublard**

☐ 5. Ça m'a pas coûté ______ !
a. **un thon** b. **une tuile** c. **une thune**

☐ 6. Mon frangin, l'en fiche pas une ______ à l'école.
a. **reine** b. **rame** c. **bosse**

☐ 7. Demain, j'dois reprend'le ______ .
a. **collier** b. **coin** c. **mur**

☐ 8. Ça coûte trop cher, ça! J'suis pas v'nu ici pour m'faire ______ !
a. **grenouiller** b. **arnaquer** c. **lézarder**

☐ 9. Laisse-moi tranquille! Tu commences à m'taper sur les ______ .
a. **nerfs** b. **tunes** c. **proprios**

☐ 10. Ma p'tite frangine, è peut pas rester assise. L'a la ______ ,celle-là!
a. **bougeotte** b. **belle étoile** c. **crèche**

☐ 11. Mon cousin, Y m'suit partout. L'est très ______ .
a. **petit** b. **collant** c. **rapide**

☐ 12. J'sais pas où il est en c'moment pasque j'l'ai ______ .
a. **engueulé** b. **claqué** c. **semé**

B. Replace the italicized word with its slang synonym from the second column. Make all necessary changes.

1. L'est *fantastique* ______________ c'film!
2. Tu peux m'prêter d'l'*argent* ______________ ?
3. Tu veux m'accompagner au *cinéma* ______________ ?
4. L'est *chère* ______________, c'te note d'hôtel!
5. J'ai *jeté* ___________ mon bouquin par la fenêtre.
6. J'dois *partir* ______________ .
7. C'est *facile* ______________ .
8. Je m'suis fait *voler* ______________ !
9. Jean, l'arriv'ra dans une *heure* ___________ .
10. *Félicitations* ______________ !
11. J'ai décidé d'*habiter* __________________ dans un hôtel pour la nuit.
12. J'vais *rester* au soleil ________________ aujourd'hui.

A. **lézarder**
B. **du gâteau**
C. **salée**
D. **chapeau**
E. **sensass**
F. **m'éclipser**
G. **arnaquer**
H. **plombe**
I. **cinoche**
J. **descendre**
K. **balancé**
L. **pognon**

C. Underline the synonym.

1. **revenons à nos moutons**:
   a. revenons à l'école — b. revenons au sujet de départ

2. **fauché**:
   a. sans argent — b. fatigué

3. **en rester baba**:
   a. être nerveux — b. être stupéfait

4. **avoir la bougeotte**:
   a. être toujours en mouvement — b. avoir de l'argent

5. **félicitations**:
   a. bonnet — b. chapeau

6. **sensass**:
   a. horrible — b. fantastique

7. **enfiler des perles**:
   a. ne rien faire — b. travailler

8. **s'éclipser**:
   a. partir vite — b. arriver vite

9. **cossard**:
   a. paresseux — b. mec

10. **roublard**:
    a. malin — b. stupide

11. **plombe**:
    a. lent — b. heure

12. **proprio**:
    a. propre — b. propriétaire

A CLOSER LOOK:
Further Use of Personal Pronouns

A. The personal pronoun "moi"

In colloquial French, the personal pronoun ***moi*** is often used to add emphasis to a command or an imperative only when the statement involves the senses or personal perception. It is used in much the same way as "just" is used in English to add emphasis to the verb that it modifies:

Regarde ça!; Look at that!
*Regarde-**moi** ça!;* Just look at that!

Goûte ça!; Taste that!
*Goûte-**moi** ça!;* Just taste that!

B. Using objective case personal pronouns to add emphasis.

In colloquial French, objective case personal pronouns (**moi**, **toi**, **lui**, **elle**, **nous**, **vous**, **eux** and **elles**) are used to: (1) emphasize the object of a statement and (2) emphasize possession.

1. To Emphasize the Object of a Statement

The object may be emphasized by simply repeating it at the end of the statement in the form of an objective case personal pronoun.

*J'peux pas l'soulever, **lui**!;* I can't lift him up, that guy!
*J'te vois, **toi**!;* I see you, you know!
*Vous m'énervez, **vous**!;* You're getting on my nerves, you!!

2. To Emphasize Possession

Possessive adjectives are used to indicate possession:

*C'est **ma** téloche;* It's my television.
*C'est **son** bouquin;* It's his book.
*C'est **notre** baraque;* It's our house.

In spoken French, the possessive adjective is emphasized by adding the preposition **à** + the appropriate objective case personal pronoun to the statement:

C'est ***ma*** *téloche* ***à moi****!;* It's my television!
C'est ***son*** *bouquin* ***à lui****!;* It's his book!
C'est ***notre*** *baraque* ***à nous****;* It's our house!

Another common way to emphasize possession is simply to reverse the order of the subject and the objective case personal pronoun. However, with this construction, the possessive adjective is replaced by the definite article **le**, **la**, **l'**, **les** or **c'**, **c't**, **c'te**:

*C't'****à lui, le*** *bouquin!;* It's his book!
*C't'****à moi, la*** *téloche!;* It's my television!
C't'***à elle, l'***apéro; It's her cocktail!
*C't'****à nous, les*** *pébrocs!;* These are our umbrellas!

*C't'****à lui, c'****bouquin!;* That's his book!
C't'***à elle, c't*** apéro; That's her cocktail!
*C't'****à nous, c'te*** *téloche!;* That's our television!

Exercises

A. Emphasize the verb using the personal pronoun "moi."

1. Regarde ça!

   ______________________________!

2. Ecoute c'te musique!

   ______________________________!

3. Sens c'gâteau!

   ______________________________!

4. Goûte ce chocolat!

   ______________________________!

5. Touche c't'étoffe!

   ______________________________!

B. Emphasize the object of the statement according to the example.

Examples:

J'te vois.	J'te parle.
J'te vois, toi.	***J'te parle, à toi.***

1. Tu l'as trouvé?

   ______________________________!

2. J't'aime bien.

   ______________________________!

3. Mais, j't'ai remboursé!

   ______________________________!

4. Y vous l'a déjà expliqué.

   ______________________________!

5. È m'l'a promis.

   ______________________________!

6. Y nous a donné un cadeau.

   ______________________________!

7. J't'ai étonné?

   ______________________________!

8. Tu l'as invitée?

   ______________________________!

9. È nous a accompagnés.

   ______________________________!

10. Y m'a beaucoup aidé.

   ______________________________!

C. Add emphasis to the possessor according to the example.

Example:

C'est sa télévision. *(lui)*

C'est sa télévision à lui.

C't'à lui, la télévision.

1. C'est son tricot. *(lui)*

______________________________!

______________________________!

2. C'est ton chien?

______________________________!

______________________________!

3. C'est sa voiture. *(elle)*

______________________________!

______________________________!

4. C'est leur appartement. *(eux)*

______________________________!

______________________________!

5. C'est son fauteuil. *(lui)*

______________________________!

______________________________!

6. C'est not'maison.

______________________________!

______________________________!

7. C'est votre enfant?

_________________________________ !

_________________________________ !

8. C'est mon pantalon.

_________________________________ !

_________________________________ !

9. C'est ta moto?

_________________________________ !

_________________________________ !

10. C'est son livre? *(elle)*

_________________________________ !

_________________________________ !

DICTATION

Test Your Aural Comprehension.

(This dictation can be found in Appendix A on page 240)

If you are following along with your cassette, you will now hear a paragraph containing many of the terms from this section. The paragraph will be read at normal conversational speed (which may actually seem fast to you at first). In addition, the words will be pronounced as you would actually hear them in a conversation, including many common reductions.

The first time the paragraph is presented, simply listen in order to get accustomed to the speed and heavy use of reductions. The paragraph will then be read again with a pause after each group of words to give you time to write down what you heard. The third time the paragraph is read, follow along with what you have written.

LEÇON HUIT

Dans le Zinc

*(In the **airplane**)*

(En Avion)

Leçon Huit

Dialogue in slang

Dans le Zinc

Anne: C'est gentil de venir me chercher à l'aéroport. J'espère que tu n'as pas eu à **poireauter** longtemps.

Paul: Non, non. Alors, **ça carbure**? Tu n'as pas l'air **dans ton assiette**.

Anne: Tu ne vas pas croire ma **déveine**. Je n'ai vraiment pas la **pêche** aujourd'hui. D'abord, j'ai pensé que j'avais **paumé** mon billet d'avion. J'ai eu du mal à le trouver quand je suis arrivée à l'aéroport! Mais enfin, je l'ai **repêché** après avoir **farfouillé** dans tous mes **bagos**. J'ai failli **me casser la gueule** en essayant de ne pas **louper** mon vol. J'ai dû **me magner le derche** parce que mon avion allait **se barrer**.

Paul: Quelle aventure! Après tout ça, tu es **arrivée** à **faire dodo** dans le **zinc**?

Anne: Tu parles! Il y avait un **type** à côté de moi qui n'arrêtait pas de **jacter**. Un vrai **moulin à paroles**.

Paul: Oh, tu **charries**!

Anne: Mais, ce n'est pas du **baratin**. Il m'a **cassé les oreilles** pendant une heure avec ses **tartines**. Il a énervé tout le monde dans le zinc! Les passagers étaient **à deux doigts** de le balancer par la fenêtre!

Lesson Eight

Translation in English

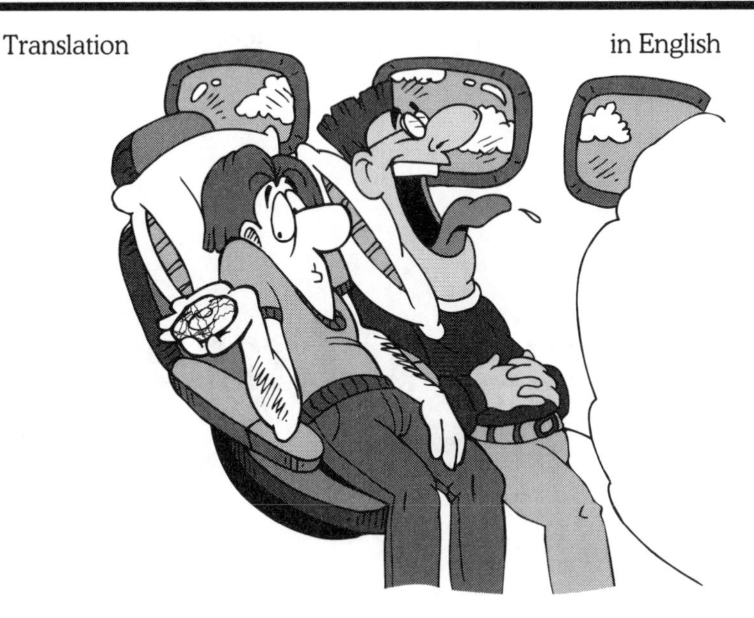

Anne: It's nice of you to come pick me up at the airport. I hope you didn't have **to wait** a long time.

Paul: Not at all. So, **what's shaking**? You look kind of **out of it**.

Anne: You're not going to believe my **lousy luck**. I'm really **not doing well** today. First off, I thought I'd **lost** my airplane ticket. I had trouble finding it when I arrived at the airport. Finally, I **found** it after **rummaging** through all my **baggage**. I almost **broke my neck** trying not to **miss** my flight. I had to **haul butt** because my plane was going **to leave**.

Paul: What an experience! After all that, did you **manage** to **sleep** in the **plane**?

Anne: You've gotta be kidding! There was a **guy** next to me who didn't stop **yacking**. A real **blabbermouth**.

Paul: Oh, you're **exaggerating**!

Anne: It's no **baloney**. He **talked my ear off** for an hour with his **endless stories**. He bothered everyone in the airplane! The passengers were **on the verge** of throwing him out the window!

Leçon Huit

Dialogue in slang as it would be spoken

Dans l'Zinc

Anne: C'est gentil de v'nir me chercher à l'aéroport. J'espère que t'as pas eu à **poireauter** longtemps.

Paul: Non, non. Alors, **ça carbure**? T'as pas l'air **dans ton assiette**.

Anne: Tu vas pas croire ma **déveine**. J'ai vraiment pas la **pêche** aujourd'hui. D'abord, j'ai pensé qu'j'avais **paumé** mon billet d'avion. J'ai eu du mal à l'trouver quand j'suis arrivée à l'aéroport! Mais enfin, j'l'ai **repêché** après avoir **farfouillé** dans tous mes **bagos**. J'ai failli **m'casser la gueule** en essayant d'ne pas **louper** mon vol. J'ai dû **m'magner l'derche** pasque mon avion, l'allait **s'barrer**.

Paul: Quelle aventure! Après tout ça, t'es **arrivée** à **faire dodo** dans le **zinc**?

Anne: Tu parles! Y avait un **type** à côté d'moi qu'arrêtait pas d'**jacter**. Un vrai **moulin à paroles**.

Paul: Oh, tu **charries**!

Anne: Mais, c'est pas du **baratin**. Y m'a **cassé les oreilles** pendant une heure avec ses **tartines**. L'a énervé tout l'monde dans l'zinc! Les passagers, z'étaient **à deux doigts** d'le balancer par la f'nêtre!

Vocabulary

à deux doigts de (être) *exp.* to be on the verge, this far away from • (lit); to be the length of two fingers away from (doing something).

example: J'étais **à deux doigts de** le tuer!

as spoken: J'étais **à deux doigts d'**le tuer!

translation: I was **this far away from** killing him!

NOTE: Although *fenêtre* is commonly used to refer to any window, the masculine noun *hublot* is the academic term used when referring to a window in an airplane or ship.

arriver à faire quelque chose *c.l.* to manage to do something • (lit); to arrive at doing something.

example: "Tu peux soulever cette caisse?"
"Je n'**y arrive** pas. C'est trop lourd."

as spoken: "Tu peux soul'ver cette caisse?"
"J'**y arrive** pas. C'est trop lourd."

translation: "Can you lift this case?"
"I can't **seem to manage it**. It's too heavy."

bagos *m.pl.* an abbreviation of "*bagages*" meaning "baggage."

example: Je n'arrive pas à trouver mes **bagos**. J'espère qu'ils ne sont pas perdus!

as spoken: J'arrive pas à trouver mes **bagos**. J'espère qu'y ~ sont pas perdus!

translation: I can't seem to find my **luggage**. I hope they're not lost!

baratin *m.* lie, nonsense, "baloney."

example: Ce qu'il te dit, c'est du **baratin**.

as spoken: C'qu'y t'dit, c'est du **baratin**.

translation: What he's telling you is a bunch of **baloney**.

NOTE: **baratiner** *v.* to talk nonsense, to B.S.

barrer (se) *v.* to leave, "to split."

example: Je suis en retard. Je dois **me barrer**!

as spoken: J'suis en r'tard. J'dois **m'barrer**.

translation: I'm late. I have **to leave**!

NOTE: The verb **barrer** literally means to strike out or cross out (a word). Therefore, the reflexive form of the verb could be loosely translated as "to strike oneself out."

SYNONYMS: *décamper • ficher/foutre le camp • mettre les voiles • mettre les bouts • prendre le large • s'arracher • se tailler*

SEE: *tailler (se), p. 10.*

carburer *v.* to be going very well • (lit); to function well (said of a carburetor).

example: Salut Jacques! **Ça carbure**?

as spoken: [no change]

translation: Hi Jack! **Everything ok**?

SYNONYMS: *ça boume? • ça gaze? • ça gazouille?*

casser la gueule (se) *exp.* to break one's "neck" • (lit); to break one's mouth or "mug."

example: Tu vas faire du ski aujourd'hui? Attention à ne pas **te casser la gueule**!

as spoken: Tu vas faire du ski aujourd'hui? Attention à n'pas **t'casser la gueule**!

translation: You're going skiing today? Be careful not **to break your neck**!

NOTE (1): **gueule** *f.* mouth or "mug" • (lit); mouth of an animal. SEE: **gueule**, *p. 94.* / **gueuleton**, *p. 8.*

NOTE (2): **casser la gueule à quelqu'un** *exp.* to break someone's neck.

example: Si tu ne me rends pas ça tout de suite, je vais **te casser la gueule**!

as spoken: Si tu m'rends pas ça tout d'suite, j'vais **t'casser la gueule**!

translation: If you don't give it back right now, I'm going **to clobber you**!

SYNONYM: **foutre une trempe à quelqu'un** *exp.* to give someone a thrashing.

casser les oreilles à quelqu'un *exp.* to talk someone's ear off • (lit); to break someone's ears.

example: Qu'elle se la boucle, à la fin! Elle **me casse les oreilles**!

as spoken: Qu'è s'la boucle, à la fin! È **m'casse les oreilles**!

translation: Would she just shut it (her mouth) already! She **talks my ear off**!

charrier *v.* to exaggerate.

example: Tu as trouvé dix millions de francs en pleine rue?! Arrête de **charrier**!

as spoken: T'as trouvé dix millions d'francs en pleine rue?! Arrête de **charrier**!

translation: You found ten million francs in the middle of the street?! Stop **exaggerating**!

dans son assiette (ne pas être) *exp.* to be out of it, out of sorts • (lit); not to be well balanced in the saddle (from horseback riding).

example: Je **ne suis pas dans mon assiette** aujourd'hui.

as spoken: J'**suis pas dans mon assiette** aujourd'hui.

translation: I'm **not myself** today.

déveine (avoir la) *f.* to have bad luck.

example: Encore un pneu crevé! C'est le deuxième aujourd'hui! J'ai la **déveine**, moi.

as spoken: [no change]

translation: Another flat tire! That's the second time today! I have **horrible luck**.

NOTE (1): **avoir de la veine** *f.* to have good luck.

NOTE (2): Note that the "*de*" is dropped in the expression *avoir la déveine* but remains in *avoir* ***de*** *la veine.*

SYNONYM (1): **manquer de pot** *exp.* to have bad luck • (lit); to lack luck • **avoir du pot** *exp.* to have good luck.

SYNONYM (2): **avoir la poisse** *exp.* • SEE: **guigne (avoir la)**, *p. 8.*

dodo (faire) *exp.* to go to sleep.

example: Je suis lessivé. Je vais **faire dodo**.

as spoken: J'suis lessivé. J'vais **faire dodo**.

translation: I'm exhausted. I'm going **to sleep**.

NOTE: This expression is actually child language yet is used in jest by adults.

VARIATION: **aller au dodo** *exp.*

farfouiller *v.* to rummage (without taking much care).

example: J'ai **farfouillé** dans tous les tiroirs pour essayer de dénicher mes clés.

as spoken: J'ai **farfouillé** dans tous les tiroirs pour essayer d'dénicher mes clés.

translation: I **rummaged** in all the drawers trying to find my keys.

jacter *v.* to speak, chatter, blab.

example: Il me casse les oreilles! Qu'est-ce qu'il **jacte**!

as spoken: Y m'casse les oreilles! Qu'est-c'qu'y **jacte**!

translation: He's talking my ear off! What a **blabbermouth**!

SYNONYM: **baver** *v.*

louper *v.* to miss.

example: J'ai **loupé** mon vol.

as spoken: [no change]

translation: I **missed** my flight.

magner le derche (se) *exp.* to hurry, "to haul one's buns" • (lit); to activate one's "derrière."

example: **Magne-toi le derche**! Nous sommes en retard!

as spoken: **Magne-toi l'derche**! Nous sommes en r'tard!

translation: **Move your butt**! We're late!

NOTE (1): **derche** *m.* slang for "*derrière*" meaning "behind."

NOTE (2): *derche* may certainly be replaced by any other synonym for buttocks such as: **arrière-train** *m.* • **brioches** *f.pl.* • **miches** *f.pl.* • **popotin** *m.* • **etc.**

moulin à paroles *m.* blabbermouth • (lit); a windmill of speech.

example: Il n'arrête pas de parler! Quel **moulin à paroles**!

as spoken: L'arrêt pas d'jacter! Quel **moulin à paroles**!

translation: He talks nonstop! What a **blabbermouth**!

SYNONYM (1): **jacteur** *m.* (from the verb *jacter* meaning "to blab").

SYNONYM (2): **jacasseur** *m.* (from the verb *jacasser* referring to the sound made by a magpie).

paumer *v.* to lose.

example (1): J'ai **paumé** mon chapeau.

as spoken: [no change]

translation: I **lost** my hat.

example (2): Je suis **paumé**! Où suis-je?

as spoken: J'suis **paumé**! Où j'suis?

translation: I'm **lost**! Where am I?

NOTE: **un paumé** *m.* a loser.

pêche (avoir la) *exp.* to be on top of the world, to be higher than a kite • (lit); to have the peach.

example: Aujourd'hui le patron m'a donné une grande augmentation! J'ai la **pêche**, moi!

as spoken: Aujourd'hui l'patron, y m'a donné une grande augmentation! J'ai la **pêche**, moi!

translation: Today the boss gave me a big raise! I'm **on top of the world**!

poireauter *v.* to wait, "to take root."

example: Ça fait une heure que tu me fais **poireauter** ici!

as spoken: Ça fait une heure qu' tu m'fais **poireauter** ici!

translation: You've been keeping me **waiting** here an hour!

NOTE: This comes from the masculine noun **poireau** meaning "leek." Therefore, **poireauter** might be translated as "to stand erect and motionless like a leek."

VARIATION: **faire le poireau** *exp.*

SYNONYM: **faire le pied de grue** *exp.* • (lit); to stand like a crane.

NOTE: The crane or *grue*, is known for standing completely motionless on one foot.

repêcher *v.* to find (something) • (lit); to "re-fish" something.

example: Mon portefeuille! Où l'as-tu **repêché**?

as spoken: Mon portefeuille! Où tu l'as **r'pêché**?

translation: My wallet! Where did you **find** it?

tartine *f.* • **1.** endless speech • **2.** big fuss • (lit); a slice of bread with a spread on top (such as butter, jam, etc.).

example (1): Elle m'a raconté toute une **tartine**.

as spoken: È m'a raconté toute une **tartine**.

translation: She told me a **long-winded story**.

example (1): Elle en a fait toute une **tartine**.

as spoken: L'en a fait toute une **tartine**.

translation: She made a **big fuss** about it.

NOTE (1): The connotation of **tartine** becomes clear when it is thought of as something "spread out" over a long period of time.

NOTE (2): **tartiner** *v.* to make a long-winded speech, to make a big deal out of nothing • (lit); to spread (out).

type *m.* guy, "dude" • (lit); type.

example: Il est beau, ce **type**-là!

as spoken: L'est beau, c'**type**-là!

translation: That guy's handsome!

SYNONYM: **mec** *m.* • SEE: *p. 52*.

NOTE: In the feminine form, **typesse**, this term becomes derogatory for a vulgar, low class woman.

zinc *m.* airplane • (lit); zinc.

example: Ce vol est trop long... six heures collé dans ce **zinc**!

as spoken: C'vol, l'est trop long...dix heures collé dans c'**zinc**!

translation: This flight is too long...ten hours stuck in this **airplane**!

NOTE: This term is now used only in jest since it originally referred to old prop planes.

Practice The Vocabulary

(Answers to Lesson 8, p. 228)

A. Complete the phrase by choosing the appropriate word from the list.

à deux doigts	**déveine**	**loupé**
arrive	**faire dodo**	**paumé**
charrier	**farfouillé**	**poireaute**
repêché	**jacte**	**tartine**

1. Le casseur, l'a ______________ dans mes affaires!

2. Allô? Nancy! J'étais ____________________ d'te téléphoner!

3. J'ai _____________ ma bague! J'pensais qu'j'l'avais ________ !

4. J'ai toujours envie d' ________________ après avoir bouffé.

5. J'ai _____________ l'bus!

6. Mais, ça fait deux heures que j'_____________ ici!

7. Arrête de ________________ . T'exagères, à la fin!

8. D'une petite histoire, y fait toute une ________________ .

9. Quelle ________________ ! J'gagne jamais!

10. J'______________ pas à soul'ver cette caisse. L'est trop lourde.

11. È m'énerve, celle-là! È __________________ sans arrêt!

B. Circle the correct synonym.

1. **baratin**: a. mensonge b. homme
2. **louper**: a. manquer b. arriver
3. **zinc**: a. avion b. valise
4. **moulin à paroles**: a. bavard b. chanson
5. **faire dodo**: a. marcher b. dormir
6. **type**: a. femme b. homme
7. **poireauter**: a. partir b. attendre
8. **se barrer**: a. partir b. arriver
9. **ça carbure**: a. ça va mal b. ça va bien
10. **paumer**: a. trouver b. perdre
11. **charrier**: a. exagérer b. partir
12. **jacter**: a. parler beaucoup b. arriver

C. Match the two columns.

☐ 1. to hurry

☐ 2. airplane

☐ 3. to be "out of it"

☐ 4. blabbermouth

☐ 5. to miss

☐ 6. to annoy someone with chatter

☐ 7. to manage to be able to do something

☐ 8. baggage

☐ 9. to hit someone

A. **ne pas être dans son assiette**

B. **arriver à faire quelque chose**

C. **bagos**

D. **casser la gueule à quelqu'un**

E. **se magner le derche**

F. **louper**

G. **moulin à paroles**

H. **zinc**

I. **casser les oreilles à quelqu'un**

A CLOSER LOOK:

The Many Colloquial Uses of "Bon"

A. To begin a conversation or wrap up a thought

Bon is frequently used as a way to begin a conversation or to wrap up one thought before beginning another. It is used in the same way as "okay" is used in English:

Bon*. Tu tournes à gauche au coin d'la rue,*
puis tu continues tout droit...

Okay. You turn left at the corner,
then you continue straight ahead...

Enfin, après avoir cherché un hôtel pendant
trois heures, j'en ai trouvé un au centre de la ville.
Bon*. Tout allait très bien jusqu'à c'que...*

Finally, after having looked for a hotel for
three hours, I found one in the center of town.
Okay. Everything was going just fine until...

B. To express anger

Bon is also used to express anger or resentment. In this case, it would be equivalent to the English word "fine" when used in anger.

Vouz voulez pas m'augmenter? ***Bon****! J'vous quitte!*
You don't want to give me a raise? Fine! I quit!

C. Bon + ben = Bon ben

Often, ***Bon ben*** is use at the end of a statement when the speaker has nothing more to say.

Bon ben*, j'm'en vais. Au r'voir!*
Well, I'm outta here. Bye!

D. Ah + bon = Ah, bon?

When used as a question, **bon** takes on the meaning of "really" when preceded by "Ah":

La semaine prochaine, j'vais aller en France.
Ah, bon?
Next week, I'm going to go to France.
Really?

Note: When used in question form, ***Ah bon*** does *not* mean "Ah, good," although this is indeed its literal translation. Therefore, it is quite correct to use **Ah, bon** upon receiving *bad* news:

Mon dab, l'est très malade.
Ah, bon?
My father is very sick.
Really?

Hier, j'ai eu un accident sérieux.
Ah, bon?
Yesterday, I was in a serious accident.
Really?

E. Pour de bon

This expression literally translates as "for good." Depending on the context, it can mean **1.** "for good" or **2.** "for real."

Pierre et Marie, y se sont quittés.
Pour de bon?
Pierre and Marie broke up.
For good?

J'ai trouvé un billet d'vingt francs dans la rue!
Pour de bon?
I found a twenty-franc bill in the street!
For real?

DICTATION

Test Your Aural Comprehension.

(This dictation can be found in Appendix A on page 241)

If you are following along with your cassette, you will now hear a paragraph containing many of the terms from this section. The paragraph will be read at normal conversational speed (which may actually seem fast to you at first). In addition, the words will be pronounced as you would actually hear them in a conversation, including many common reductions.

The first time the paragraph is presented, simply listen in order to get accustomed to the speed and heavy use of reductions. The paragraph will then be read again with a pause after each group of words to give you time to write down what you heard. The third time the paragraph is read, follow along with what you have written.

LEÇON NEUF

Un Coup de Fil

(A **telephone call**)

(Au Téléphone)

Dialogue in slang

Au Bigophone

Jeanne: Ben alors? Elle a dit quoi cette fois?

Margot: Oh, j'**en ai soupé** de ses **bobards**! Elle a **dégoisé** pendant toute une heure pour me dire comment elle va devenir actrice, grande chanteuse, mannequin international, **et patati et patata**. Quelle **crâneuse**!

Jeanne: C'est toujours la même **rengaine** et franchement, je **m'en fiche comme de ma première chaussette**. Elle réussira une carrière comme ça **quand les poules auront des dents**.

Margot: Elle n'a pas la **bosse** du chant. Ce n'est pas **dans ses cordes**.

Jeanne: Et avec les **guibolles** qu'elle a, elle doit être **timbrée** de penser qu'elle peut devenir mannequin! Sa **tignasse** est horrible, elle a un gros **pif** qui bouffe toute sa **tronche peinturlurée**, et des **chocottes** cradingues. Un vrai **boudin**, quoi!

Margot: Et **ça saute aux yeux** qu'elle n'est pas **bien roulée**.

Jeanne: Tu ne trouves pas qu'on n'est pas gentilles?

Margot: Il faut **appeler un chat un chat**. C'est une **bonne à rien**.

Jeanne: Tu sais...en **y regardant à deux fois**, peut-être qu'elle pourrait réussir comme actrice. Si jamais on fait un **remake** de La Femme de Frankenstein, **c'est dans la poche**!

Lesson Nine

Translation in English

Jeanne: So? What did she say this time?

Margot: Oh, I've **had it** with her **baloney**! She **rattled on** for an entire hour telling me how she's going to become an actress, big singer, international model, **and blah blah blah**. What a **showoff**!

Jeanne: It's always the **same old story** and frankly, I **don't give a hoot**. She'll succeed at getting a career like that **when donkeys fly**.

Margot: She doesn't have the **knack** for singing. It's not **up her alley**.

Jeanne: And with the **legs** she has, she must be **nuts** to think that she can become a model! Her **hair** is horrible, she has a big **honker** that eats her entire **painted up face**, and filthy **teeth**. A real **ugo**!

Margot: And **it's obvious** that she doesn't have a **good figure**.

Jeanne: Don't you think we're not being very nice?

Margot: Let's **call a spade a spade**. She's a **good-for-nothing**.

Jeanne: You know... **come to think of it**, maybe she could make it as an actress. If they ever decide to do a **remake** of The Bride of Frankenstein, **it's in the bag**!

Leçon Neuf

Dialogue in slang as it would be spoken

Au Téléphone

Jeanne: Ben alors? L'a dit quoi cette fois?

Margot: Oh, j'**en ai soupé** d'ses **bobards**! L'a **dégoisé** pendant toute une heure pour me dire comment è va dev'nir actrice, grande chanteuse, mannequin international, **et patati et patata**. Quelle **crâneuse**!

Jeanne: C'est toujours la même **rengaine** et franchement, j'**m'en fiche comme de ma première chaussette**. È réussira une carrière comme ça **quand les poules auront des dents**.

Margot: L'a pas la **bosse** du chant. C'est pas **dans ses cordes**.

Jeanne: Et avec les **guibolles** qu'elle a, è doit êt' **timbrée** d'penser qu'è peut dev'nir mannequin! Sa **tignasse**, l'est horrible, l'a un gros **pif** qui bouffe toute sa **tronche peinturlurée**, et des **chocottes** cradingues. Un vrai **boudin**, quoi!

Margot: Et **ça saute aux yeux** qu'elle est pas **bien roulée**.

Jeanne: Tu trouves pas qu'on est pas gentilles?

Margot: Faut **appeler un chat un chat**. C't'une **bonne à rien**.

Jeanne: Tu sais...en **y regardant à deux fois**, p't-êt'qu'è pourrait réussir comme actrice. Si jamais on fait un **remake** de La Femme de Frankenstein, **c'est dans la poche**!

Vocabulary

bien roulée (être) *adj.* (describing a woman) to have a good body • (lit); to be rolled (together) well.

example: Elle fait de la gymnastique. C'est pour ça qu'elle est **bien roulée**!

as spoken: È fait d'la gymnastique. C'est pour ça qu'elle est **bien roulée**!

translation: She works out. That's why she's got a **great body**!

NOTE: **baraqué (être)** *adj.* (describing a man) to be buffed out.

bon(ne) à rien *exp.* good-for-nothing, loser.

example: Il ne fait rien toute la journée. Quel **bon à rien**!

as spoken: Y fait rien toute la journée. Quel **bon à rien**!

translation: He doesn't do a thing all day. What a **good-for-nothing**!

bosse de quelque chose (avoir la) *exp.* to be gifted for something • (lit); to have the bump of something.

example: Elle a **la bosse du** piano.

as spoken: [no change]

translation: She has a **knack** for the piano.

boudin *m.* ugly girl • (lit); blood sausage.

example: C'est la fiancée de Marc? Oh, quel **boudin**!

as spoken: C'est la fiancée d'Marc? Oh, quel **boudin**!

translation: That's Mark's fiancée? What an **ugo**!

SYNONYM: **mocheté** *f.* (from the slang verb *moche* meaning "ugly").

"Ça saute aux yeux" *c.l.* said of something obvious • (lit); it jumps to the eyes.

example: Quelle maison! **Ça saute aux yeux** qu'il est riche!

as spoken: [no change]

translation: What a house! It's **obvious** that he's rich!

chocottes *f.pl.* teeth.

example: Tu as de très belles **chocottes**, toi. Elles sont si blanches!

as spoken: T'as d'très belles **chocottes**, toi. È sont si blanches!

translation: You have really pretty **teeth**. They're so white!

SYNONYM: **dominos** *m.pl.*

coup de fil *m.* telephone call, a ring, a jingle • (lit); a blow on the line.

example: Je te donne un **coup de fil** plus tard.

as spoken: J'te donne un **coup d'fil** plus tard.

translation: I'll give you a **ring** later.

ALSO: **au bout du fil (être)** *exp.* to be on the phone (lit); to be at the end of the line.

crâneuse *f.* conceited woman or girl.

example: Elle pense qu'elle est supérieure au reste du monde. C'est une vraie **crâneuse**.

as spoken: È pense qu'elle est supérieure au reste du monde. C't'une vraie **crâneuse**.

translation: She thinks she's superior to the rest of the world. She's a real **conceited person**.

NOTE: **crâneur** *m.* conceited man or boy.

dans la poche (être) *exp.* to be a sure bet • (lit); to be in the pocket.

example: Je suis certain qu'il va t'engager parce que tu as les meilleures qualifications! Ne t'inquiète pas. C'**est dans la poche**.

as spoken: J'suis certain qu'y va t'engager pasque t'as les meilleures qualifications! ~ T'inquiète pas. C'**est dans la poche**.

translation: I'm sure he's going to hire you because you have the best qualifications! Don't worry. It's **a sure bet**!

SYNONYM: **cousu d'avance (être)** *exp.* • (lit); it's already sewn up.

dans les cordes de quelqu'un (être) *exp.* to be up one's alley • (lit) to be in one's ropes.

example: Je ne sais pas jouer du piano. Ce n'est pas **dans mes cordes**.

as spoken: J'sais pas jouer du piano. C'est pas **dans mes cordes**.

translation: I can't play the piano. It's just not **up my alley**!

dégoiser *v.* to talk a lot, to spout off at the mouth.

example: Il est fatigant, lui! Il a **dégoisé** pendant toute une heure au téléphone!

as spoken: L'est fatigant, lui! L'a **dégoisé** pendant toute une heure au bout du fil!

translation: He's so tiring! He **rattled on an on** for an entire hour on the telephone!

SYNONYM (1): **baver** *v.* • (lit); to drool.

SYNONYM (2): **jacter** *v.* • SEE: *p. 161*.

et patati et patata *exp.* and blah, blah, blah.

example: Elle a dégoisé pendant une heure sur ses études, sur ses projets, sur ses amis, **et patati et patata**.

as spoken: L'a dégoisé pendant une heure sur ses études, sur ses projets, sur ses amis, **et patati et patata**.

translation: She rattled on for an entire hour about her studies, about her projects, about her friends, **and blah, blah, blah**.

fiche comme de sa première chaussette (s'en) *exp.* not to care at all about something • (lit); to care about something as much as about one's first sock.

example: Carole m'a dit que Marcel parle de moi derrière mon dos. Eh bien, je **m'en fiche comme de ma première chaussette**!

as spoken: Carole, è m'a dit que Marcel, y parle de moi derrière mon dos. Eh bien, j'**m'en fiche comme de ma première chaussette**!

translation: Carole told me that Marcel is talking about me behind my back. Frankly, I **couldn't care less**.

VARIATION: **fiche comme de sa première chemise (s'en)** *exp.* • (lit); to care about something as much as about one's first shirt.

guibolles *f.pl.* legs.

example: Ça fait six heures qu'on n'arrête pas de danser! J'ai mal aux **guibolles**, moi!

as spoken: Ça fait six heures qu'on ~ arrête pas d'danser! J'ai mal aux **guibolles**, moi!

translation: We've been dancing nonstop for six hours! My **legs** hurt!

SYNONYM: **cannes** *f.pl.* • (lit); canes.

peinturluré(e) (être) *adj.* to wear gobs of makeup, to wear "war paint" • (lit); *peinturlurer:* to paint (a building, etc. using all of the colors of the rainbow).

example: Tu as vu la nouvelle employée? Ce n'est pas possible comme elle est **peinturlurée**, cette nana!

as spoken: T'as vu la nouvelle employée? C'est pas possible comme elle est **peinturlurée**, c'te nana!

translation: Did you see the new employee? It's unreal how that girl's face is **painted** up!

SYNONYM: **badigeonner** *v.* • (lit); to color-wash (a wall, etc.).

ALSO: **badigeon** *m.* makeup, "war paint" • (lit); color-wash.

pif *m.* nose, "honker."

example: Ce gamin a un grand **pif** comme celui de son vieux.

as spoken: C'gamin, l'a un grand **pif** comme celui d'son vieux.

translation: That kid has a big **honker** like his father's.

SYNONYM: **blair** *m.* • SEE: *p. 115.*

quand les poules auront des dents *exp.* (humorous) never, "when pigs fly" • (lit); when hens have teeth.

example: Je l'inviterai à dîner **quand les poules auront des dents**! Je ne peux pas le blairer!

as spoken: J'l'invit'rai à dîner **quand les poules auront des dents**! J'peux pas l'blairer!

translation: I'll invite him to dinner **when pigs fly**! I can't stand him!

rengaine *f.* repetitious story.

example: C'est toujours la même **rengaine**. Je l'invite chez moi et il me dit qu'il est trop occupé.

as spoken: C'est toujours la même **rengaine**. J'l'invite chez moi et y m'dit qu'il est trop occupé.

translation: It's always the same **old story**. I invite him to my house and he tells me that he's too busy.

soupé (en avoir) *exp.* to be fed up, to have had enough of it.

example: C'est la troisième fois que le patron me donne du boulot à faire pendant le weekend! J'**en ai soupé** de lui!

as spoken: C'est la troisième fois que l'patron, y m'donne du boulot à faire pendant l'weekend! J'**en ai soupé** d'lui!

translation: This is the third time the boss has given me work to do over the weekend. I'**ve had it** with him!

SYNONYM (1): **marre (en avoir)** *exp.* • SEE: *p. 8.*

SYNONYM (2): **ras le bol (en avoir)** exp. (pronounced: "ralbol") • (lit); to have had it up to the edge of the bowl.

tignasse *f.* a mop of hair.

example: Elle n'a pas honte de sortir avec une telle **tignasse**? On dirait qu'elle ne se coiffe jamais!

as spoken: L'a pas honte de sortir avec une telle **tignasse**? On dirait qu'è s'coiffe jamais!

translation: Isn't she ashamed to go out with that **hair**? It looks like she's never brushed it!

SYNONYM: **tifs** *m.pl.* • SEE: *p. 124*.

timbré(e) (être) *adj.* to be crazy, cracked • (lit); to have one's bell rung.

example: Il conduit dans le mauvais sens! Il doit être **timbré**, celui-là!

as spoken: Y conduit dans l'mauvais sens! Y doit êt' **timbré**, c'ui-là!

translation: He's driving in the wrong direction! He must be **nuts**!

SYNONYM (1): **cinglé(e) (être)** *adj.*

SYNONYM (2): **sonné(e) (être)** *adj.* • (lit); to be rung.

SYNONYM (3): **fêlé(e) (être)** *adj.* (from the verb fêler meaning "to crack").

tronche *f.* head; face, "mug" • (lit); log.

example: Avec une telle **tronche**, elle ne pourra jamais devenir actrice!

as spoken: Avec une telle **tronche**, è pourra jamais dev'nir actrice!

translation: With such a **mug**, she'll never be able to be an actress!

SYNONYM: **poire** *f.* • (lit); pear.

Practice The Vocabulary

(Answers to Lesson 9, p. 230)

A. CONTEXT EXERCISE
Choose the best idiom from the right column that goes with the phrase in the left column.

☐ 1. È devrait dev'nir manequin.

☐ 2. Y doit êt'danseur.

☐ 3. Tu crois pas qu'elle a b'soin de chirurgie plastique?

☐ 4. Y m'a parlé d'sa carrière, de ses problèmes personnels, de ses vacances.

☐ 5. J'sais pas jouer au tennis.

☐ 6. Quel beau sourire qu'il a, Michel!

☐ 7. Tu veux qu'j'l'invite chez nous?!

☐ 8. È croit qu'elle est supérieure au reste du monde.

☐ 9. J'suis sûr que tu vas gagner.

☐ 10. Y parle tout seul dans la rue.

A. **Et patati et patata.**

B. **L'a un pif gigantesque, celle-là!**

C. **C'est pas dans mes cordes.**

D. **L'est super bien roulée!**

E. **L'a des guibolles très musclées, lui.**

F. **Faut dire qu'il a de très belles chocottes.**

G. **C'est dans la poche.**

H. **Absolument pas! Quand les poules auront des dents.**

I. **Quelle crâneuse!**

J. **J'crois qu'il est timbré.**

B. CROSSWORD

Fill in the crossword puzzle on the opposite page by choosing the correct word(s) from the list below.

bosse	**crâneuse**	**pif**
boudin	**dégoiser**	**poche**
chocottes	**dents**	**roulée**
chaussette	**guibolles**	**soupé**
cordes	**patata**	**yeux**

Across

17. ______ *v.* to talk a lot, to spout off at the mouth.

29. **fiche comme de sa première ______ (s'en)** *exp.* not to care at all about something.

41. **bien ______ (être)** *adj.* to have a good body.

45. ______ **(en avoir)** *exp.* to be fed up, to have had enough of it.

49. ______ *m.* nose, "honker."

58. **"Ça saute aux ______"** *c.l.* said of something obvious.

Down

9. ______ *f.pl.* legs.

12. ______ *f.pl.* teeth.

15. ______ **de quelque chose (avoir la)** *exp.* to be gifted for something.

16. ______ *f.* conceited woman or girl.

17. **quand les poules auront des ______** *exp.* (humorous) never, "when pigs fly."

24. **et patati et ______** *exp.* and blah, blah, blah.

29. **dans les ______ de quelqu'un (être)** *exp.* to be up one's alley.

34. ______ *m.* ugly girl.

47. **dans la ______ (être)** *exp.* to be a sure bet.

CROSSWORD PUZZLE

C. Choose the correct phrase that best fits the idiom.

1. C'est pas dans mes **cordes**.
   - ☐ a. J'adore la musique.
   - ☐ b. J'sais pas l'faire.
   - ☐ c. J'sais l'faire.

2. T'as des **guibolles** musclées, toi.
   - ☐ a. Tu fais d'la culture physique (*bodybuilding*)?
   - ☐ b. Tu joues du piano?
   - ☐ c. T'es médecin?

3. C'te nana, l'est toujours **peinturlurée**.
   - ☐ a. È s'rait plus belle si è portait du maquillage.
   - ☐ b. On dirait qu'è porte un masque.
   - ☐ c. È parle sans arrêt!

4. C'est un **bon à rien**.
   - ☐ a. L'est très énergique.
   - ☐ b. On peut toujours compter sur lui.
   - ☐ c. On peut jamais compter sur lui.

5. J'**en ai soupé** de lui!
   - ☐ a. On a beaucoup trop bouffé!
   - ☐ b. J'veux plus l'voir!
   - ☐ c. Ça me plaît toujours d'le voir.

6. C't'un **boudin**!
   - ☐ a. Qu'est-ce qu'elle est jolie!
   - ☐ b. Qu'est-ce qu'elle est moche!
   - ☐ c. Qu'est-ce qu'elle est intelligente!

7. L'est très **bien roulée** pasqu'è...
   - ☐ a. bouffe constamment.
   - ☐ b. chante tous les jours.
   - ☐ c. fait d'la gymnastique.

8. Y n'fait que **dégoiser**!
   - ☐ a. L'arrête pas d'parler.
   - ☐ b. Y parle presque jamais.
   - ☐ c. Y parle jamais à personne..

A CLOSER LOOK:

The Interjective Use of the Relative and Interrogative Pronoun "Quoi"

A. "Quoi" used euphemistically

Often, we are asked to give our opinion about something of a personal nature such as the clothes someone is wearing, an accomplishment, an idea, etc. There is usually a slight pause as we search for just the right non-offensive word to use. In French, once the speaker has found the exact word to use, the relative pronoun ***quoi*** will follow as an interjection. This is an *extremely* popular usage of ***quoi***. (The actual thoughts of the speaker are shown in parentheses.)

(Quelle robe affreuse!)
C'est ta robe neuve, ça? Elle est tellement...spéciale, ***quoi****!*
Is that your new dress? It's so...special!

(Quel acteur horrible!)
Comme acteur, vous êtes...dans une catégorie à part, ***quoi****!*
As an actor, you are...in a league of your own!

B. "Quoi" used to indicate emotion

When the speaker is either overcome with emotion or great sentiment, ***quoi*** is commonly for emphasis:

(Quel spectacle stupéfiant!)
Le spectacle, il était absolument...fantastique, ***quoi****!*

(Je crois que je vais pleurer!)
C'que vous avez fait pour moi était si...gentil, ***quoi****!*

C. "Quoi" used to indicate impatience

Quoi is also used at the end of a statement to indicate impatience. In this instance, ***quoi*** is used in much the same way as "already" in English:

C'est toujours toi qui es assis à l'avant. Cette fois, c'est mon tour, ***quoi****!*
You always get to ride in the front. This time, it's my turn, already!

On doit y êt'dans cinq minutes! Dépêche-toi, ***quoi****!*
We have to be there in five minutes! Hurry up, already!

SYNONYM: When used to indicate impatience, ***enfin*** is a common replacement for ***quoi*** and can be used interchangeably:

C'est toujours toi qui es assis à l'avant. Cette fois, c'est mon tour, ***enfin****!*
On doit y êt'dans cinq minutes! Dépêche-toi, ***enfin****!*

Practice "Quoi"

A. Translate the phrases into French using the relative pronoun "quoi" as an interjection.

Example:

The dinner was... special!
(euphemism) Le dîner, il était... spécial, quoi!

1. *Your dog has a lot of... personality!*

   *(euphemism)*______________________________________!

2. *Your shirt is so... bright!*

   *(euphemism)*______________________________________!

3. *Stop that, already!*

   *(impatience)*______________________________________!

4. *I love your house! It's so... warm!*

   (emotion)____!

5. *The dinner was absolutely... sensational!*

   (emotion)____!

6. *Let's go, already!*

   (impatience)______________________________________!

7. *The ceremony was extremely... moving!*

   (emotion)____!

8. *The decor in your home is very... unique!*

   (euphemism)______________________________________!

DICTATION

Test Your Aural Comprehension.

(This dictation can be found in Appendix A on page 242)

If you are following along with your cassette, you will now hear a paragraph containing many of the terms from this section. The paragraph will be read at normal conversational speed (which may actually seem fast to you at first). In addition, the words will be pronounced as you would actually hear them in a conversation, including many common reductions.

The first time the paragraph is presented, simply listen in order to get accustomed to the speed and heavy use of reductions. The paragraph will then be read again with a pause after each group of words to give you time to write down what you heard. The third time the paragraph is read, follow along with what you have written.

LEÇON TEN

J'ai la Crève!

*(I'm **sick**!)*

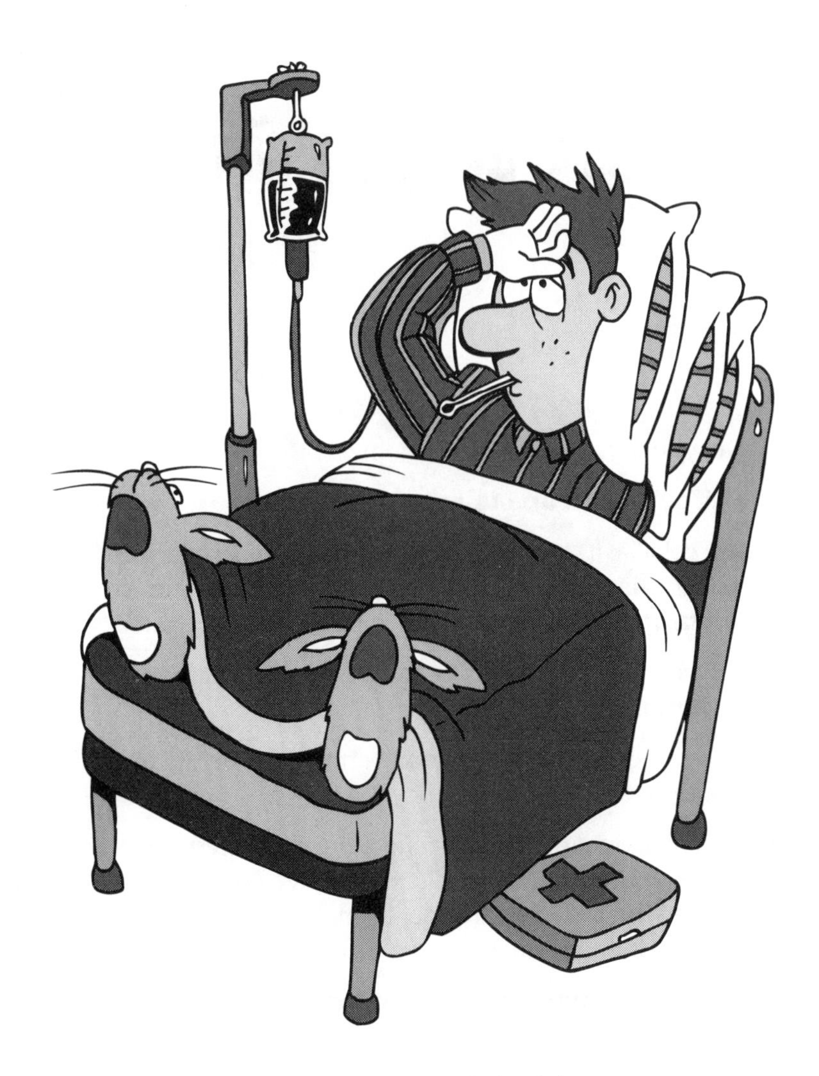

(Un Grand Malade)

Leçon Dix

Dialogue in slang

J'ai la Crève!

Marie: Salut Robert. Ben, où il est, Thomas?

Robert: Il dit qu'il a **attrapé la crève**, qu'il est **mal fichu**.

Marie: Oh, celui-là, il se croit toujours **à l'article de la mort**. La semaine dernière, il pensait qu'il allait **clamser** d'une crise de **battant**! Je n'ai jamais vu un hypochondriaque pareil!

Robert: Les médecins **prennent la tangente** quand ils le voient **débarquer**!

Marie: L'hôpital doit avoir un **pageot** permanent pour lui avec son **blaze** dessus!

Robert: Il y a quand même quelque chose qui **ne tourne pas rond**: il tousse constamment mais n'arrête pas de fumer. Puis, il **en fait toute une salade** parce qu'il a mal aux **éponges**. Il va **flipper** au point où il va se faire une **belle corbuche**.

Marie: **Un de ces quat'**, un **tranche-lard** va lui dire de **passer sur le billard**. Je suis sûre que ça va le **requinquer** et **en moins de deux**!

Lesson Ten

Translation in English

Marie: Hi Bob. So, where's Tom?

Robert: He says he **caught his death**, that he's really **sick**.

Marie: Oh, that guy always thinks he's **at death's door**. Last week, he thought he was gonna **croak** from a **heart** attack! I've never seen such a hypochondriac!

Robert: All the doctors must **haul outta there** when they see him **coming**!

Marie: The hospital must have a permanent **bed** for him with his **name** on it!

Robert: And yet, there is still **something wrong with him**: he coughs nonstop but doesn't stop smoking. Then, he **makes a big deal about** how his **lungs** hurt. He's gonna **flip out** to the point where he's going to end up with **one heck of an ulcer**.

Marie: One of these days, a **surgeon** is going to tell him to **hop up on the operating table**. I'm sure that'll help him **perk up** and **in no time flat**!

Leçon Dix

Dialogue in slang as it would be spoken

J'ai la Crève!

Marie: Salut Robert. Ben, où il est, Thomas?

Robert: Y dit qu'il a **attrapé la crève**, qu'il est **mal fichu**.

Marie: Oh, c'ui-là, y s'croit toujours **à l'article de la mort**. La s'maine dernière, il pensait qu'il allait **clamser** d'une crise de **battant**! J'ai jamais vu un hypocondriaque pareil!

Robert: Les médecins **prennent la tangente** quand y l'voient **débarquer**!

Marie: L'hôpital doit avoir un **pageot** permanent pour lui avec son **blaze** dessus!

Robert: Y a quand même quèque chose qui **tourne pas rond**: y tousse constamment mais arrête pas d'fumer. Puis, il **en fait toute une salade** pasqu'il a mal aux **éponges**. Y va **flipper** au point où y va s'faire une **belle corbuche**.

Marie: **Un d'ces quat'**, un **tranche-lard**, y va lui dire de **passer su'l'billard**. J'suis sûre que ça va l'**requinquer** et **en moins d'deux**!

Vocabulary

à l'article de la mort (être) *c.l.* to be at death's door • (lit); to be at the critical point of death.

example: Je ne me sens pas bien. Je suis sûr que je suis **à l'article de la mort**!

as spoken: Je m'sens pas bien. J'suis sûr que j'suis **à l'article de la mort**!

translation: I don't feel well. I'm sure I'm **at death's door**!

attraper la crève *exp.* to catch a terrible cold • (lit); to catch one's death.

example: J'ai **attrapé la crève** en vacances.

as spoken: [no change]

translation: I **caught a terrible cold** on my vacation.

NOTE: **crever** *v.* to die.

example: Je **crève** de faim!

as spoken: J'**crève** de faim!

translation: I'm **dying** of hunger!

battant *m.* heart, "ticker" • (lit); beater.

example: Mon grand-père a quatre-vingt-dix (90) ans et pourtant, il a le **battant** très solide.

as spoken: Mon grand-père, l'a quat'-vingt-dix (90) ans et pourtant, l'a l'**battant** très solide.

translation: My grandfather is ninety years old and yet, he has a very strong heart.

NOTE: This comes from the verb **battre** meaning "to beat."

SYNONYM: **palpitant** *m.* • (lit); palpitater.

belle/beau *adj.* considerable, "quite a..." • (lit); pretty/handsome.

example: Tu te feras une **belle** hernie si tu essaies de soulever ça!

as spoken: Tu t' f'ras une **belle** hernie si t'essaies d'soul'ver ça!

translation: You'll give yourself **quite a** hernia if you try to lift that!

blaze *m.* name.

example: Quel est son **blaze**?

as spoken: Son **blaze**, c'est quoi?

translation: What's his **name**?

NOTE (1): This is from the masculin noun *blason* meaning "coat of arms."

NOTE (2): The noun **blaze** is considered extremely slangy and is primarily used only by younger people.

"Ça ne tourne pas rond" *exp.* "Something's wrong," "I'm not donig well" • (lit); "It's not rolling smoothly."

example: **Ça ne tourne pas rond** pour moi en ce moment. Je n'ai pas de boulot et tous mes amis m'ont lâché(e).

as spoken: **Ça ~ tourne pas rond** pour moi en c'moment. J'ai pas d'boulot et tous mes amis, y m'ont lâché(e).

translation: Things are not going well for me these days. I've got no job and all my friends have dropped me.

clamser *v.* to die, "to croak."

example: Qu'il fait chaud! Je vais **clamser**!

as spoken: Qu'y fait chaud! J'vais **clamser**!

translation: Is it ever hot! I'm gonna **die**!

SYNONYM (1): **passer l'arme à gauche** *exp.*

SYNONYM (2): **crever** *v.*

corbuche *f.* ulcer.

example: Je me sens des aigreurs. J'espère que je n'ai pas de **corbuche**!

as spoken: Je m'sens des aigreurs. J'espère qu' j'ai pas d'**corbuche**!

translation: I have heartburn. I hope I don't have an **ulcer**!

débarquer *v.* to arrive without notice • (lit); to disembark.

example: Il a **débarqué** chez moi à minuit!

as spoken: L'a **débarqué** chez moi à minuit!

translation: **Without any notice, he arrived** at my house at midnight!

en moins de deux *exp.* quickly • (lit); in less than two (seconds).

example: J'arrive **en moins de deux**.

as spoken: J'arrive **en moins d'deux**.

translation: I'll be there **in a flash**.

éponges *f.pl.* lungs • (lit); sponges.

example: Pourquoi tu fumes? Ce n'est pas bon pour les **éponges**.

as spoken: Pourquoi tu fumes? C'est pas bon pour les **éponges**.

translation: Why do you smoke? It's not good for the **lungs**.

flipper *v.* (from the same English verb) to go crazy, to flip out.

example: J'ai horreur d'aller à New York parce qu'il y a trop de monde. Les foules me font **flipper**!

as spoken: J'ai horreur d'aller à New York pasqu'y a trop d'monde. Les foules, è m'font **flipper**!

translation: I hate going to New York because there are too many people. Crowds make me **freak out**!

SYNONYM (1): **perdre les pédales** *exp.* • (lit); to lose the pedals.

SYNONYM (2): **perdre la boule** *exp.* • (lit); to lose the ball.

NOTE: **boule** *f.* head • (lit); ball.

mal fichu (être) *adj.* to be sick • (lit); to be badly put together.

example: Qu'est-ce qu'il y a? Tu as l'air **mal fichu** aujourd'hui.

as spoken: Qu'est-c'qu'~ y a? T'as l'air **mal fichu** aujourd'hui.

translation: What's wrong? You look **sick** today.

pageot *m.* bed.

example: Ton **pageot** est trop mou. C'est pour ça que tu as mal au dos.

as spoken: Ton **pageot**, l'est trop mou. C'est pour ça qu' t'as mal au dos.

translation: Your **bed** is too soft. That's why your back is sore.

NOTE (1): **se pageoter** *v.* to go to bed.

NOTE (2): **se dépageoter** *v.* to get out of bed.

SYNONYM (1): **plumard** *m.* • (lit); that which is made of feathers or *"plumes"* • SEE: **plumard**, *p. 53.*

SYNONYM (2): **pieu** *m.* • (lit); stake or post.

passer sur le billard *exp.* to undergo surgery • (lit); to go onto the billiard table.

example: Demain tu **passes sur le billard**? Mais qu'est-ce que tu as?

as spoken: Demain, tu **passes su' l'billard**? Mais qu'est-c'que t'as?

translation: Tomorrow you're **going in for surgery**? What's wrong with you?

prendre la tangente *exp.* to slip away without being seen • (lit); to take the tangent.

example: Je m'ennuie ici. Je vais **prendre la tangente**.

as spoken: J'm'ennuie ici. J'vais **prend' la tangente**.

translation: I'm bored here. I'm going **to sneak out**.

requinquer *v.* to perk up.

example: Ces vitamines vont te **requinquer** tout de suite.

as spoken: Ces vitamines, è vont t'**requinquer** tout d'suite.

translation: These vitamins will **perk** you **up** right away.

toute une salade (en faire) *exp.* to make a big deal about something • (lit); to make a big salad over something.

example: Je n'ai pas mis ma chambre en ordre et ma vieille **en a fait toute une salade**!

as spoken: J'ai pas mis ma chambre en ordre et ma vieille, l'**en a fait toute une salade**!

translation: I didn't clean up my bedroom and my old lady **made a big stink about it**.

SYNONYM: **toute une tartine (en faire)** exp. • SEE: *p.163*.

tranche-lard *m.* (humorous) surgeon • (lit); fat-slicer.

example: Mon frangin est **tranche-lard**.

as spoken: Mon frangin, c't'un **tranche-lard**.

translation: My brother's a **surgeon**.

un de ces quat' *exp.* a common abbreviation for *un de ces quatre matins* meaning "one of these days" • (lit); one of these four (mornings).

example: Un de ces quat', je vais devenir **riche**!

as spoken: Un d'ces quat', j'vais dev'nir **riche**!

translation: One of these days, I'm gonna be **rich**!

Practice The Vocabulary 

(Answers to Lesson 10, p. 229)

A. Were the following words used correctly or incorrectly?

1. **Un d'ces quat'**, j'vais dev'nir vedette.
   ☐ correct ☐ incorrect

2. J'crois qu'j'ai **attrapé la crève**. Je m'sens très bien.
   ☐ correct ☐ incorrect

3. Mon père, c't'un **tranche-lard**. Y travaille dans une charcuterie.
   ☐ correct ☐ incorrect

4. J'vais bien dormir ce soir. Aujourd'hui, je m'suis acheté un nouveau **pageot**.
   ☐ correct ☐ incorrect

5. J'vais louper mon bus! J'dois **prend' la tangente**!
   ☐ correct ☐ incorrect

6. Marcel, y m'a accompagné au ciné aujourd'hui. Hier soir, il a **clamsé**.
   ☐ correct ☐ incorrect

7. «Quel est ton **blaze**?» «J'm'appelle Henri.»
   ☐ correct ☐ incorrect

8. Je m'sens **mal fichu** aujourd'hui. J'ai jamais été en aussi bonne forme.
   ☐ correct ☐ incorrect

B. Underline the appropriate word that best completes the phrase.

1. Jean, l'a attrapé la (**crève**, **salade**, **tangente**). J'l'ai jamais vu aussi malade!

2. Ton oncle, l'est mort d'une crise de (**pageot**, **battant**, **tranche-lard**)? Mais y faisait d'la danse aérobique trois fois par semaine!

3. Pour le moment, j'dors par terre pasque j'ai pas d'(**blaze**, **billard**, **pageot**).

4. T'es malade? T'as l'air mal (**fichu**, **habillé**, **coiffé**) aujourd'hui.

5. Antoine, l'a (**débarqué**, **clamsé**, **mal fichu**) ce matin. Les funérailles, è z'auront lieu d'main.

6. Mais pourquoi t'arrêtes pas d'fumer? C'est pour ça que t'as mal aux (**pageots**, **blazes**, **éponges**)!

7. En c'moment, avec la crise économique, ça tourne pas (**carré**, **rectangle**, **rond**).

8. Ma mère, l'en a fait toute une (**tarte**, **soupe**, **salade**) pasque j'ai pas fait mon lit.

9. Mon cours de français, y commence dans cinq minutes! J'prends la (**ligne**, **tangente**, **cercle**)!

10. J'peux pas manger la cuisine mexicaine. C'est trop épicé pour moi à cause de ma (**corbuche**, **salade**, **tangente**).

C. Choose the most appropriate definition of the words in boldface.

☐ 1. Quand ma mère va découvrir que j'ai cassé sa montre, è va **flipper**!
☐ a. to do backflips
☐ b. turn over in her grave
☐ c. flip out

☐ 2. L'est grand, ton **pageot**.
☐ a. bed
☐ b. house
☐ c. car

☐ 3. J'ai d'mauvaises nouvelles. Sylvie, elle est **à l'article de la mort**.
☐ a. in the newspaper
☐ b. quitting her job
☐ c. at death's door

☐ 4. Quand y m'a vu v'nir, l'a **pris la tangente**.
☐ a. left in a hurry
☐ b. ran up to me
☐ c. gave me a hug

☐ 5. J'étais tellement malade que j'pensais qu'j'allais **clamser**!
☐ a. to laugh
☐ b. to die
☐ c. to leave

☐ 6. Prends c'médicament. Ça va te **requinquer**.
☐ a. perk up
☐ b. calm down
☐ c. knock out

☐ 7. Demain, j'dois **passer su'l'billard**.
☐ a. play pool
☐ b. work all day
☐ c. undergo surgery

☐ 8. T'as vu Henri? L'a **débarqué** c'matin.
☐ a. arrived
☐ b. left
☐ c. quit his job

A CLOSER LOOK I:

The Omission of the Possessive Adjective

A. In an imperative or command

In French, possessive adjectives (**mon**, **ma**, **mes**, **ton**, **ta**, **tes**, **son**, **sa**, **ses**, **notre**, **nos**, **votre**, **vos**, **leur** and **leurs**) are used to modify the noun they precede:

Voici ma mère.
This is my mother.

Regarde ma nouvelle voiture!
Look at my new car!

A common construction used by French natives is one where the possessive adjective is dropped in an imperative or command (and replaced with a definite article along with a personal pronoun) *only* if an action is being taken on a physical attribute (head, back, arm, etc.). For example, in the following, action is *not* being taken on the physical attribute; therefore, the possessive adjective remains:

Regarde mon dos.
Look at my back.

Remarque mes cheveux.
Notice my hair.

In the following, an action *is* being taken on the physical attribute:

*Masse-**moi le** dos.*
Massage my back.

*Coupe-**moi les** cheveux.*
Cut my hair.

*Tiens-**moi la** main.*
Hold my hand

Verb	POSSESSIVE ADJECTIVE	Noun
Masse	**mon**	*dos.*
Coupe	**mes**	*cheveux.*

Verb	PERSONAL PRONOUN	DEFINITE ARTICLE	Noun
Masse -	**moi**	**le**	*dos.*
Coupe -	**moi**	**les**	*cheveux.*

B. In a statement

The possessive adjective may also be dropped in a statement *only* if an action is being taken on the physical attribute. In the following, an action is *not* being taken:

Je regarde son dos.
I'm looking at his/her back

Elle remarque ses cheveux.
She's noticing his/her hair.

In the following, an action *is* being taken on the physical attribute:

Je ***lui*** *masse* ***le*** *dos.*
I'm massaging his/her back.

Elle ***me*** *coupe* ***les*** *cheveux.*
She's cutting my hair.

The possessive adjective takes the form of the appropriate personal pronoun and is placed before the verb, and a definite article is placed before the object. The same applies to pronominal verbs (when the action is being done to oneself):

I wash my hands = *Je* ***me*** *lave* ***les*** *mains.*
She brushes her hair = *Elle* ***se*** *brosse* ***les*** *cheveux.*

Subject	Verb	**POSSESSIVE ADJECTIVE**	Object
Je	*masse*	***son***	*dos.*
Elle	*coupe*	***mes***	*cheveux.*

Subject	**PERSONAL PRONOUN**	Verb	**DEFINITE ARTICLE**	Object
Je	***lui***	*masse*	***le***	*dos.*
Elle	***me***	*coupe*	***les***	*cheveux.*

C. In the past tense (passé composé)

In the past tense as well, the personal pronoun is placed after the subject (just as it was in the present tense):

Subject	Personal Pronoun	**VERB**	Definite Article	Object
Je	*lui*	***masse***	*le*	*dos.*
Elle	*me*	***coupe***	*les*	*cheveux.*

Subject	Personal Pronoun	**AVOIR**	**PAST PARTICIPLE**	Definite Article	Object
Je	*lui*	***ai***	***massé***	*le*	*dos.*
Elle	*m'*	***a***	***coupé***	*les*	*cheveux.*

D. In the past tense using pronominal verbs

The construction here is much like that of "C" above with the exception that, as with all reflexive verbs, the past participle is conjugated with *être:*

Subject	Personal Pronoun	**ÊTRE**	**PAST PARTICIPLE**	Definite Article	Object
Je	*me*	***suis***	***lavé***	*les*	*mains.*
Elle	*s'*	***est***	***cassé***	*la*	*jambe.*

Practice the Omission of the Possessive Article

A. Rewrite the imperatives, omitting the underlined possessive article.

1. Gratte son cou. *(Scratch his neck)*

   ______________________________.

2. Essuie ton menton. *(Wipe your chin)*

   ______________________________.

3. Brosse mes cheveux. *(Brush my hair)*

   ______________________________.

4. Arrache ma dent. *(Pull my tooth)*

   ______________________________.

5. Touche son épaule *(Touch his shoulder)*

   ______________________________.

6. Tiens mon bras. *(Hold my arm)*

   ______________________________.

7. Serre ma main. *(Shake my hand)*

   ______________________________.

8. Lave ta figure. *(Wash your face)*

   ______________________________.

B. Rewrite the statement, omitting the underlined possessive article.

1. Y touche <u>mon</u> épaule. *(He's touching my shoulder)*

 ______________________________________ .

2. J'ai gratté <u>son</u> cou. *(I scratched his neck)*

 ______________________________________ .

3. J'ai cassé <u>son</u> bras. *(I broke his arm)*

 ______________________________________ .

4. Elle a pincé <u>mon</u> nez. *(She pinched my nose)*

 ______________________________________ .

5. J'peigne <u>ses</u> cheveux. *(I'm combing his/her hair)*

 ______________________________________ .

6. Le dentiste, il a arraché <u>ses</u> dents. *(The dentist pulled out his/her teeth)*

 ______________________________________ .

7. Elle a caressé <u>ma</u> joue. *(She caressed my face)*

 ______________________________________ .

8. Ça fend mon cœur. *(That just breaks my heart)*

_______________________________________ .

9. Je lave mes dents. *(I'm brushing my teeth)*

_______________________________________ .

10. È maquille ses yeux. *(She's making up her [own] eyes)*

_______________________________________ .

11. È maquille ses yeux. *(She's making up her [someone else's] eyes)*

_______________________________________ .

12. L'a chuchoté à son oreille. *(He whispered in his/her ear)*

_______________________________________ .

A CLOSER LOOK II:
Personal Pronouns when Offering and Asking for Favors

A. In an imperative or command

A construction similar to that shown in GRAMMAR IA also holds true when the imperative or command is in reference to a favor or service, e.g., "Hold this for me," "Carry this suitcase for me," etc. In this case, the object and personal pronoun change places and ***pour*** is omitted since it is built into the construction:

Verb	Object	POUR	Personal Pronoun
Tiens	*ça*	***pour***	***moi.***
Porte	*la valise*	***pour***	***moi.***

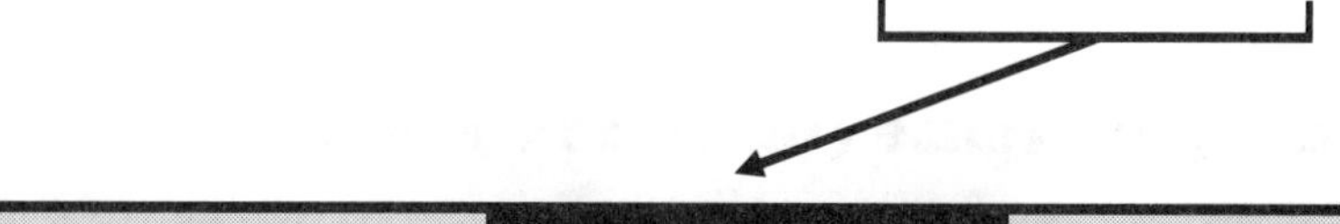

Verb	PERSONAL PRONOUN	Object
Tiens -	***moi***	*ça.*
Porte -	***moi***	*la valise.*

B. In reference to a favor or service

When a statement is in reference to a favor or service, the personal pronoun is placed before the verb and ***pour*** is once again omitted since it is built into the construction. This is similar to the construction in GRAMMAR IB on page 202.

Subject	Verb	Object	POUR	PERSONAL PRONOUN
Je	*tiens*	*la porte*	***pour***	***toi*.**
Je	*porte*	*la valise*	***pour***	***toi*.**

Subject	PERSONAL PRONOUN	Verb	Object
Je	***te***	*tiens*	*la porte.*
Je	***te***	*porte*	*la valise.*

NOTE: This construction is also used when asking a question:

Je te tiens la porte?
May I hold the door for you?

Je te porte la valise?
May I carry the suitcase for you?

C. In the past tense (passé composé)

In the past tense, the personal pronoun is placed after the subject, just as it is in the present tense.

Subject	Personal Pronoun	VERB	Object
Je	*te*	***tiens***	*la porte.*
Je	*te*	***porte***	*la valise.*

Subject	Personal Pronoun	AVOIR	PAST PARTICIPLE	Object
Je	*t'*	***ai***	***tenu***	*la porte.*
Je	*t'*	***ai***	***porté***	*la valise.*

Practice Offering and Asking for Favors

A. Rewrite the imperative according to the example.

Example:

Tiens la porte pour moi.
Tiens-moi la porte.

1. Tiens ça pour moi. *(Hold this for me)*

   ____.

2. Porte le manteau pour elle. *(Carry the coat for her)*

   ____.

3. Ouv'la porte pour lui. *(Open the door for him)*

   ____.

4. Soulève la valise pour moi. *(Lift the suitcase for me)*

   ____.

5. Vérifie cette liste pour nous. *(Verify this list for us)*

   ____.

6. Coupe cette ficelle pour moi. *(Cut this string for me)*

   ____.

7. Lave ces tasses pour elle. *(Wash these cups for her)*

   ____.

8. Change c't'ampoule pour lui. *(Change this light bulb for him)*

   ____.

9. Ferme la porte pour moi. *(Close the door for me)*

   ____.

10. Répare la voiture pour nous. *(Fix the car for us)*

    ____.

B. Rewrite the sentence according to the example.

Example:

Il a peint la maison pour moi. *(He painted the house for me)*
Il m'a peint la maison.

1. J'tiens les livres pour toi? *(Shall I hold the books for you?)*

   ______________________________.

2. Il a porté l'manteau pour moi. *(He carried my coat for me)*

   ______________________________.

3. Il a ouvert la porte pour elle. *(He opened the door for her)*

   ______________________________.

4. Je soulève la valise pour toi? *(May I lift the suitcase for you)*

   ______________________________.

5. J'ai vérifié la liste pour lui. *(I verified the list for him)*

   ______________________________.

6. J'coupe la ficelle pour toi? *(May I cut the string for you)*

   ______________________________.

7. J'ai lavé la tasse pour toi. *(I washed the cup for you)*

   ______________________________.

8. Il a changé l'ampoule pour elle. *(He changed the light bulb for her)*

   ______________________________.

9. Elle a fait la cuisine pour moi. *(She cooked for me)*

   ______________________________.

10. Il a réparé la voiture pour nous. *(He fixed the car for us)*

    ______________________________.

DICTATION
Test Your Aural Comprehension.

(This dictation can be found in Appendix A on page 243)

If you are following along with your cassette, you will now hear a paragraph containing many of the terms from this section. The paragraph will be read at normal conversational speed (which may actually seem fast to you at first). In addition, the words will be pronounced as you would actually hear them in a conversation, including many common reductions.

The first time the paragraph is presented, simply listen in order to get accustomed to the speed and heavy use of reductions. The paragraph will then be read again with a pause after each group of words to give you time to write down what you heard. The third time the paragraph is read, follow along with what you have written.

REVIEW EXAM FOR LESSONS 6-10

(Answers to Review, p. 224)

A. Underline the appropriate word that best completes the phrase.

1. Oh, la (**girafe**, **vache**, **chienne**)! L'est jolie, ta baraque!

2. Si ma vieille, è sait qu'j'ai cassé son vase, j'suis (**fric**, **frangin**, **frit**).

3. J'ai entendu dire qu' t'as réussi à tous tes exams! (**Casquette**, **Bonnet**, **Chapeau**)!

4. Y fait rien toute la journée. C't'un vrai (**cossard**, **cinoche**, **potasse**).

5. J'ai beaucoup d'(**crèche**, **pognon**, **bouquins**) sur moi. J'suis riche!

6. Y flotte encore! Quel temps d'(**chat**, **chien**, **canard**)!

7. Le film, y commence dans dix minutes! Faut s'(**poireauter**, **repérer**, **barrer**)!

8. J'suis fatigué pasque j'ai pas pu (**pioncer**, **poireauter**, **farfouiller**) toute la nuit. Les voisins, y faisaient trop d'bruit.

9. Brigitte, è m'a parlé pendant toute une plombe de son rendez-vous avec Marc. Franchement, j'm'en fiche comme de ma première (**chaussure**, **cravate**, **chaussette**).

10. J'peux pas chanter, moi. C'est pas dans mes (**ficelles**, **cordes**, **lignes**).

B. CONTEXT EXERCISE
Fill in the letter corresponding to the correct phrase in the right column.

☐	1. T'aimes lire?	A. È doit êt'**cinglée**!
☐	2. T'as vu c'te nana-là? È parle toute seule!	B. J'ai pas d'**pognon**.
☐	3. Y fait rien toute la journée.	C. J'dois **m'éclipser**.
☐	4. J'peux pas t'accompagner au ciné ce soir.	D. Mais, oui! C'est pour ça qu' j'achète un nouveau **bouquin** chaque semaine.
☐	5. J'suis en r'tard.	E. Quel **moulin à paroles**!
☐	6. L'arrête pas d'parler!	F. J'ai pas pu **pioncer** toute la nuit.
☐	7. J'suis fatigué.	G. J'dois **passer su' l'billard**.
☐	8. J'arrive pas à trouver mon portefeuille.	H. J'espère que j'l'ai pas **paumé** quèque part!
☐	9. J'peux pas chanter, moi.	I. Je sais. C't'un vrai **cossard**, lui.
☐	10. Demain j'vais à l'hôpital.	J. C'**est pas dans mes cordes**.

C. CROSSWORD

Step 1: Fill in the blanks with the appropriate word(s) from the list below.
Step 2: Using your answers, fill in the crossword puzzle on the opposite page.

blairer	**gâteau**	**salade**
bobards	**louper**	**soupé**
crève	**nerfs**	**tangente**
doigts	**poche**	**vache**

ACROSS

16. Nicolas, c'est ton ami?! Oh, j'peux pas l'__________ !

18. Jeanne, è semble très triste aujourd'hui. J'ai l'impression qu'elle est à deux __________ d'chialer!

25. C'est pas difficile. Au contraire! C'est du __________ !

31. Oh, la __________ ! C'est extraordinaire!

34. J'suis pas allé au boulot aujourd'hui pasque j'ai la __________ .

39. J'en ai __________ d'ses questions stupides!

DOWN

7. J'me barre tout d'suite. J'veux pas __________ mon bus.

10. Faut pas croire c'qu'è t'dit. È raconte que des __________ .

15. Quand l'flic, y s'est approché, le voleur, l'a pris la __________ !

22. Tu vas sûrement obtenir le rôle. C'est dans la __________ .

24. Ma cousine, l'en a fait toute une __________ quand j'ai oublié son anniversaire.

30. Arrête de m'suiv' partout! Tu me tapes sur les __________ , toi!

CROSSWORD PUZZLE

D. Choose the correct definition of the word(s) in boldface.

1. **quand les poules auront des dents:**
   a. never b. sometimes c. once

2. **requinquer:**
   a. to tire b. to perk up c. to eat

3. **déveine:**
   a. bad luck b. good luck c. large crowd

4. **tif:**
   a. hair b. big nose c. ugly face

5. **s'éclipser:**
   a. to go to sleep b. to arrive c. to leave

6. **dénicher:**
   a. to leave b. to laugh c. to find

7. **poireauter:**
   a. to leave b. to laugh c. to wait

8. **paumer:**
   a. to lose b. to arrive c. to look

9. **c'est du gâteau:**
   a. it's hard b. it's easy c. it's impossible

10. **pognon:**
    a. money b. food c. intense fear

ANSWERS TO LESSONS 1-10

LEÇON UN - *Il Flotte Encore!*

Practice the Vocabulary

A. 1. C
2. B
3. H
4. G
5. F
6. I
7. J
8. D
9. A
10. E

B. 1. dingue
2. caille
3. guigne
4. cloche
5. bouffe
6. fric
7. carrément
8. boudin

C. 1. F
2. A
3. G
4. C
5. B
6. H
7. I
8. D
9. E
10. J

A CLOSER LOOK I: *Practice Using Contractions*

A. 1. T'as
2. J'te
3. J'comprends • c'que
4. J'vais • l'voir
5. T'entends pas
6. J'veux • prend'
7. J'dois
8. J'peux • prend' • l'métro • j'me/je m'
9. j'vais • mett'
10. J'pars • d'suite • êt'
11. J'ai pas
12. J'peux pas • l'faire

B. Aujourd'hui, je vais me lever de bonne heure pour passer la journée en ville. Je dois arriver vers midi pour déjeuner avec mes amis Irène et Jacques à notre café préféré. J'aime bien ce café parce que les prix ne sont pas astronomiques! Après, on va aller au parc prendre une glace! Si on a le temps, on va pousser jusqu'au jardin du Luxembourg.

A CLOSER LOOK II: *Exercises*

A.
1. c't'un
2. y a
3. c'ui-là
4. faut
5. l'est
6. quèque chose
7. y parle
8. qu'est
9. y avait
10. è rit

B.
1. L'a • J'dois • prend'
2. Y • parc' • y' • s'tirer
3. C't'un
4. Y a • d'
5. m' • s'te plaît
6. Z'ont (or Y z'ont)
7. J'crois • è • m' • d' • que
8. J'ai • d'
9. J'sais • c'qu'y • m'
10. Y • pasqu'y

LEÇON DEUX - *Quel Boui-Boui!*

Practice the Vocabulary

A.
1. b
2. a
3. b
4. b
5. a
6. a
7. b
8. b
9. b
10. a

B. **CROSSWORD PUZZLE**

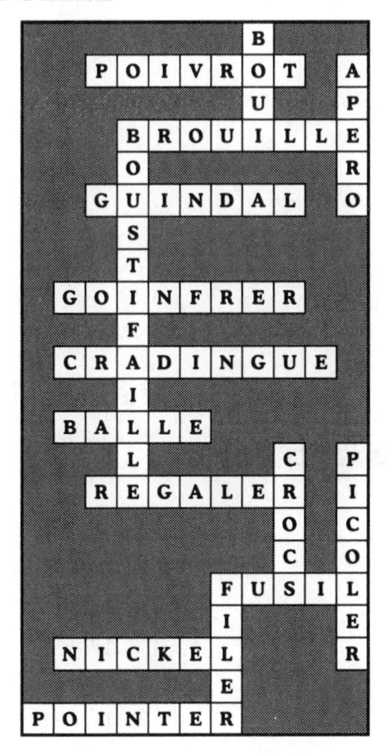

C.
1. badigoinces
2. bourrée
3. douloureuse
4. cradingues
5. régale
6. poivrot
7. brouille-ménage
8. fusil
9. boui-boui
10. me goinfrer
11. balles
12. nickel

A CLOSER LOOK I: *Practice Asking a Question*

A.
1. Qui tu vas aider?
2. Quand tu veux partir?
3. Quelle heure il est?
4. Pourquoi t'aimes pas ça?
5. Comment y va aller à la plage?
6. T'écris quoi?
7. Y vient d'où?
8. T'as combien d'pantalons?
9. Tu désires m'accompagner?
10. Tu prends l'autobus?
11. Tu sais conduire?
12. T'aimes ça?

B. 1. A qui tu vas parler du boui-boui?
2. È regarde qui?
3. Tu veux quoi?
4. Tu vas commander quoi?
5. A qui tu vas parler?
6. T'as hérité de quoi?
7. Elle a combien d'enfants?
8. Où y va s'goinfrer ce soir?
9. Avec qui è va picoler?
10. Y va laver quoi?

LEÇON TROIS - *On a Piqué Ma Téloche!*

Practice the Vocabulary

A. 1. agrafer
2. lourde
3. écopé
4. baraque
5. fourré
6. salut
7. flicaille
8. plumard
9. balader
10. placard
11. bousillé
12. planquer

B. 1. I
2. B
3. D
4. C
5. H
6. E
7. A
8. G
9. J
10. F

C. 1. L'a piqué mon vélo, lui.
2. J'veux regarder la téloche.
3. J'ai bousillé ma montre.
4. V'là l'casseur!
5. Tu veux encarrer?
6. Tu connais c'mec?
7. Si tu veux plus ta guitare, tu pourrais la mettre au clou!
8. Z'ont/y z'ont radiné à quelle heure?
9. Tu veux t'balader après l'dîner?
10. J'suis lessivé.

A CLOSER LOOK I: *Exercises*

A. 1. a. Ce gâteau, l'est délicieux.
b. L'est délicieux, c'gâteau.

2. a. Suzanne, l'est très jolie.
b. L'est très jolie, Suzanne.

3. a. Le dîner, l'est gâché.
b. L'est gâché, l'dîner.

4. a. Cette robe, è m'va comme un gant.
b. È m'va comme un gant, cette robe.

5. a. Le film, l'était fantastique.
b. L'était fantastique, le film.

6. a. Ma mère, è m'appelle.
b. È m'appelle, ma mère.

7. a. Les jours, y passent vite.
b. Y passent vite, les jours.

8. a. Cette voiture, l'est toute neuve.
b. L'est toute neuve, cette voiture.

9. a. Mon frère, l'est très grand.
b. L'est très grand, mon frère.

10. a. Serge, y t'demande au téléphone.
b. Y t'demande au téléphone, Serge.

B. 1. Tu fais c'bordel pourquoi?
2. T'as bousillé quoi?
3. Tu vas acheter quelle baraque?
4. Y l'a piqué quand?
5. T'essaies d'planquer qui?
6. Tu t'es carapaté pourquoi?
7. Y va parler à la flicaille quand?
8. T'as combien de téloches?
9. Z'ont/y z'ont radiné avec qui?
10. Tu vas t'balader où?
11. T'es lessivé pourquoi?
12. Z'ont/y z'ont fourré qui en prison?

LEÇON QUATRE - *La Joie d'Être Bouchon*

Practice the Vocabulary

A.
1. C
2. G
3. F
4. M
5. J
6. K
7. L
8. B
9. H
10. D
11. A
12. I
13. E

B.
1. a
2. c
3. c
4. b
5. b
6. a
7. a
8. a
9. b
10. a
11. a

C. **FAMILY TREE**

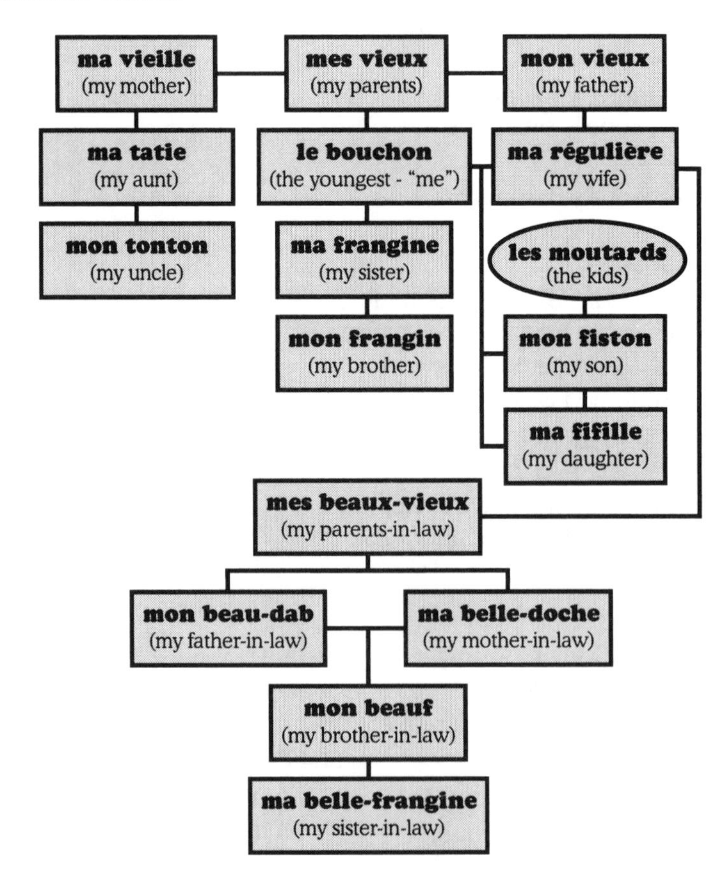

Practice c'te, un peu, ben , and alors

A.
1. Ecoute un peu cette musique!
2. Ecoute c'te musique!
3. Ecoute un peu c'te musique!
4. Ben écoute!
5. Ecoute donc!
6. Ben oui!
7. Oui alors!
8. Ben oui alors!
9. Regarde c't'architecture!
10. Regarde un peu ce livre!
11. Regarde un peu c'livre!
12. Cours donc!
13. Ben viens donc!
14. Ben regarde un peu c'te baraque!

LEÇON CINQ - *La Grande Boum*

Practice the Vocabulary

A.
1. clope
2. fringué
3. nana / brancher
4. boule
5. marrant
6. trouille
7. bigle
8. schlingue
9. déjantes
10. bile
11. boum

B.
1. clodo
2. jeter
3. boyaux
4. rond
5. amygdales
6. clope
7. pommes
8. brancher
9. pince
10. trouille
11. draguer
12. marrant
13. gargue

C.
1. A
2. K
3. E
4. B
5. D
6. I
7. M
8. H
9. J
10. C
11. G
12. F

A CLOSER LOOK 1: *Exercises*

A.
1. moi
2. lui
3. elle
4. toi
5. vous
6. toi
7. moi
8. lui
9. elle
10. ça
11. nous
12. ça

B.
1. Pourquoi ça
2. Où ça
3. Comment ça
4. Pourquoi ça
5. Qui ça
6. Où ça
7. Pourquoi ça
8. Qui ça
9. Pourquoi ça
10. Quand ça

REVIEW EXAM FOR LESSONS 1-5

Practice the Vocabulary

A.
1. a, c, d
2. a, c, d
3. b, c, d
4. a, b, c
5. b, d
6. c, d
7. a, b, c
8. a, b, d
9. a, b, c
10. b, d
11. a, d
12. b, c, d

B.
1. schlingue
2. clope
3. dingue
4. nana
5. cailler
6. moutards
7. marrant
8. mauvais poil
9. baraque
10. pommes
11. trouille
12. file

C. **CROSSWORD PUZZLE**

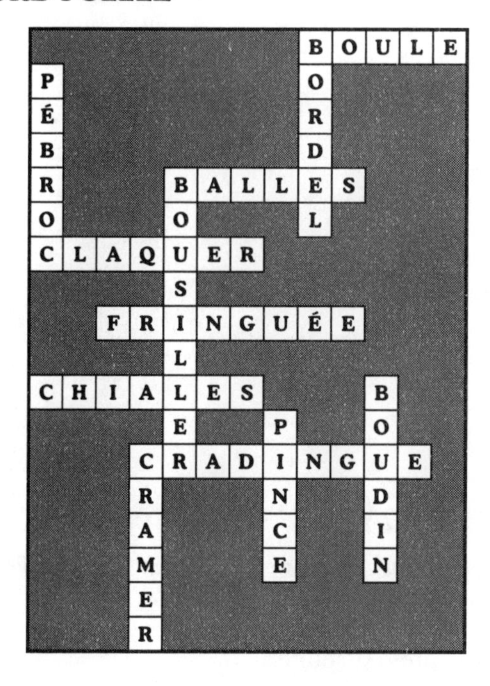

D.
1. L
2. A
3. K
4. J
5. D
6. G
7. E
8. B
9. C
10. F
11. I
12. H

LEÇON SIX - *Le Chouchou du Prof*

Practice the Vocabulary

A.
1. bosser
2. blairer
3. zieuter
4. bouquin
5. casser
6. la vache
7. moche
8. calé
9. étendre
10. tifs, merlan, déboiser

B.
1. cinglé
2. potasser, étendre
3. prof
4. déboiser, melon
5. fiche, paquet
6. plancher, galerie
7. chouchou
8. potaches
9. calée, maths
10. méganote
11. séché

C.
1. a
2. c
3. a
4. b
5. c
6. b
7. b
8. a
9. c
10. a
11. b
12. c

A CLOSER LOOK 1:
Practice Using The Present Tense To Indicate Future

A.
1. On s'voit d'main, alors?
2. J'te l'donne après l'déjeuner.
3. On l'fait plus tard.
4. On en discute demain.
5. J'te la présente à la soirée.
6. Y te l'rend ce soir.
7. J'viens t'chercher à 8h.
8. Ce soir, è lui fait une grande surprise.
9. C't'après-midi, on fête ton anniversaire.
10. J'te passe un coup d'fil demain.

LEÇON SEPT - *La Vie de Cossard*

Practice the Vocabulary

A.
1. b
2. c
3. a
4. a
5. c
6. b
7. a
8. b
9. a
10. a
11. b
12. c

B. 1. E
2. L
3. I
4. C
5. K
6. F
7. B
8. G
9. H
10. D
11. J
12. A

C. 1. b
2. a
3. b
4. a
5. b
6. b
7. a
8. a
9. a
10. a
11. b
12. b

A CLOSER LOOK 1: *Exercises*

A. 1. Regarde-moi ça!
2. Ecoute-moi c'te musique!
3. Sens-moi c'gâteau!
4. Goûte-moi c'chocolat!
5. Touche-moi c't'étoffe!

B. 1. Tu l'as trouvé, lui?
2. J't'aime bien, toi.
3. Mais, j't'ai remboursé, toi!
4. Y vous l'a déjà expliqué, à vous.
5. È m'l'a promis, à moi!
6. Y nous a donné un cadeau, à nous.
7. J't'ai étonné, toi?
8. Tu l'as invitée, elle?
9. È nous a accompagnés, nous.
10. Y m'a beaucoup aidé, moi.

C. 1. C'est son tricot à lui.
C't'à lui, l'tricot.

2. C'est ton chien à toi?
C't'à toi, l'chien?

3. C'est sa voiture à elle?
C't'à elle, la voiture?

4. C'est leur appartement à eux?
C't'à eux, l'appartement?

5. C'est son fauteuil à lui?
C't'à lui, le fauteuil?

6. C'est not'maison à nous.
C't'à nous, la maison.

7. C'est votre enfant à vous?
C't'à vous, l'enfant?

8. C'est mon pantalon à moi.
C't'à moi, l'pantalon.

9. C'est ta moto à toi?
C't'à toi, la moto?

10. C'est son livre à elle?
C't'à elle, le livre?

LEÇON HUIT - *Dans le Zinc*

Practice the Vocabulary

A. 1. farfouillé
2. à deux doigts
3. repêché, paumé
4. faire dodo
5. loupé
6. poireaute
7. charrier
8. tartine
9. déveine
10. arrive
11. jacte

B. 1. a
2. a
3. a
4. a
5. b
6. b
7. b
8. a
9. b
10. b
11. a
12. a

C. 1. E
2. H
3. A
4. G
5. F
6. I
7. B
8. C
9. D

LEÇON NEUF - *Un Coup de Fil*

Practice the Vocabulary

A. 1. D
2. E
3. B
4. A
5. C
6. F
7. H
8. I
9. G
10. J

B. **CROSSWORD PUZZLE**

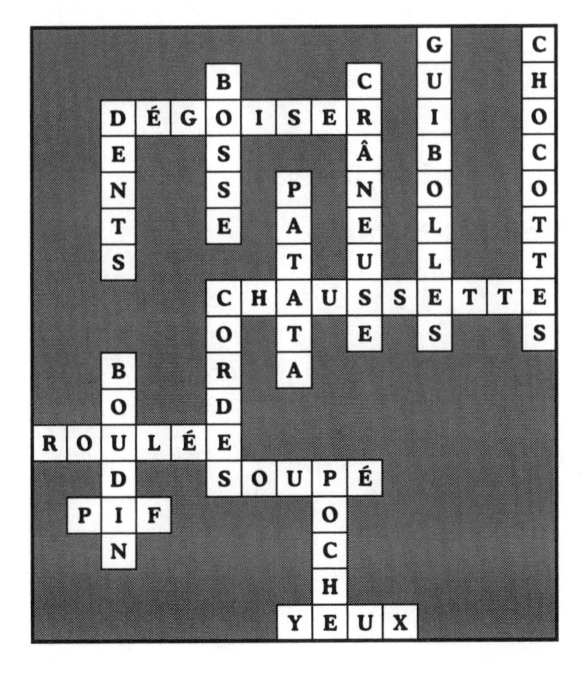

C. 1. b
2. a
3. b
4. c
5. b
6. b
7. c
8. a

A CLOSER LOOK: *Practice "Quoi"*

A. 1. Ton chien, l'a beaucoup d'personnalité, quoi!
2. Ta chemise, l'est si colorée, quoi!
3. Arrête, quoi!
4. J'adore vot'maison! L'est si chaleureuse, quoi!
5. Le dîner, l'était absolument sensas, quoi!
6. Partons, quoi!
7. La cérémonie, l'était extrêmement émouvante, quoi!
8. Le décor chez vous, l'est très unique, quoi!

LEÇON DIX - *J'ai la Crève!*

Practice the Vocabulary

A. 1. correct
2. incorrect
3. incorrect
4. correct
5. correct
6. incorrect
7. correct
8. incorrect

B. 1. crève
2. battant
3. pageot
4. fichu
5. clamsé
6. éponges
7. rond
8. salade
9. tangente
10. corbuche

C. 1. c
2. a
3. c
4. a
5. b
6. a
7. c
8. a

A CLOSER LOOK I:
Practice The Omission of the Possessive Adjective

A. 1. Gratte-lui l'cou.
2. Essuie-toi l'menton.
3. Brosse-moi les cheveux.
4. Arrache-moi la dent.
5. Touche-lui l'épaule.
6. Tiens-moi l'bras.
7. Serre-moi la main.
8. Lave-toi la figure.

B. 1. Y m'touche l'épaule.
2. Je lui ai gratté l'cou.
3. Je lui ai cassé l'bras.
4. È m'a pincé l'nez.
5. Je lui peigne les cheveux.
6. Le dentiste, y lui a arraché les dents.
7. È m'a caressé la joue.
8. Que ça m'fend l'cœur!
9. J'me brosse les dents.
10. È s'maquille les yeux.
11. È lui maquille les yeux.
12. Y lui a chuchoté à l'oreille.

A CLOSER LOOK: *Practice Offering and Asking for Favors*

A.
1. Tiens-moi ça.
2. Porte-lui c'manteau.
3. Ouv'-lui la porte.
4. Soulève-moi la valise.
5. Vérifie-nous cette liste.
6. Coupe-moi cette ficelle
7. Lave-lui cette tasse.
8. Change-lui c't'ampoule.
9. Ferme-moi la f'nêtre.
10. Répare-nous la voiture.

B.
1. J'te tiens les livres?
2. Y m'a porté l'manteau.
3. Y lui a ouvert la porte.
4. J'te soulève la valise?
5. Je lui ai vérifié la liste.
6. J'te coupe la ficelle?
7. J't'ai lavé la tasse.
8. Y lui a changé l'ampoule.
9. È m'a fait la cuisine.
10. Y nous a réparé la voiture.

REVIEW EXAM FOR LESSONS 6-10

Practice the Vocabulary

A.
1. vache
2. frit
3. chapeau
4. cossard
5. pognon
6. chien
7. barrer
8. pioncer
9. chaussette
10. cordes

B.
1. D
2. A
3. I
4. B
5. C
6. E
7. F
8. H
9. J
10. G

C. **CROSSWORD PUZZLE**

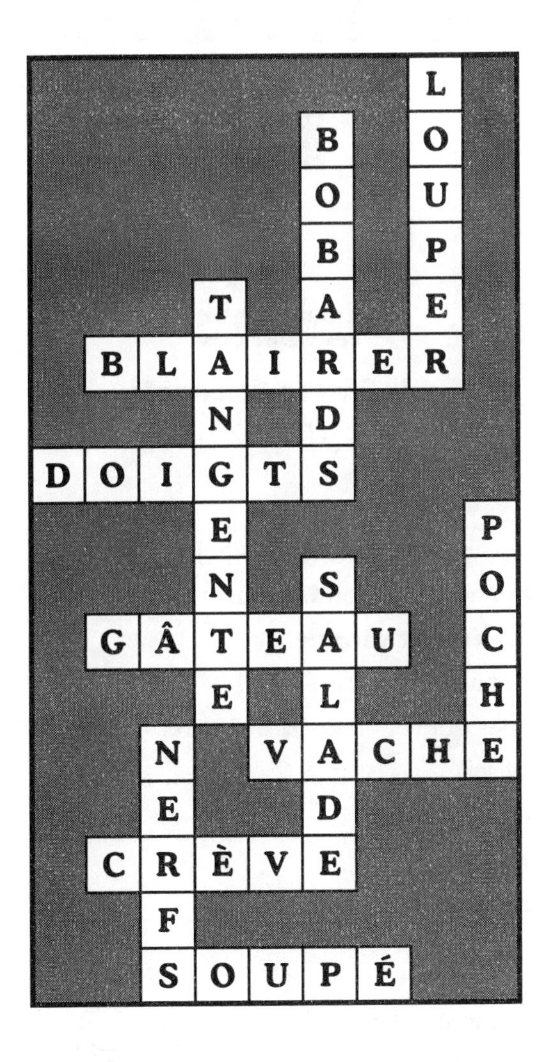

D.
1. a
2. b
3. a
4. a
5. c
6. c
7. c
8. a
9. b
10. a

APPENDIX

-Dictations-

Leçon Un

Il Flotte Encore!
(It's raining again!)

[Using reductions, as heard on the audiotape]

1. J'viens d'**claquer** tout mon **fric** sur la **bouffe**.
2. J'dois êt' **carrément dingue**.
3. Quel **gueuleton** ça va être!
4. On **s'tire** pour trouver un **coin peinard**.
5. C'est **génial**, ici!
6. Y commence à **flotter**!
7. J'ai pas d'**pébroc**.
8. **J'en r'viens pas**, moi!

[As you would see it written]

1. Je viens de **claquer** tout mon **fric** sur la **bouffe**.
2. Je dois être **carrément dingue**.
3. Quel **gueuleton** ça va être!
4. On **se tire** pour trouver un **coin peinard**.
5. C'est **génial**, ici!
6. Il commence à **flotter**!
7. Je n'ai pas de **pébroc**.
8. **Je n'en reviens pas**, moi!

Leçon Deux

Quel Boui-Boui!

(What a dive!)

[Using reductions, as heard on the audiotape]

1. Quel **boui-boui**! C'est **cradingue** ici!
2. C'**resto**, l'est **d'première**.
3. J'commence à avoir les **crocs**.
4. J'vais **m'goinfrer** c'soir.
5. J'm'**en pourlèche les badigoinces** d'avance.
6. Deux cents **balles** pour du **brouille-ménage**?
7. La **boustifaille** à c'resto, ça doit êt' le **coup d'fusil**!
8. C'est moi qui **régale**.

[As you would see it written]

1. Quel **boui-boui**! C'est **cradingue** ici!
2. Ce **resto** est **de première**.
3. Je commence à avoir les **crocs**.
4. Je vais **me goinfrer** ce soir.
5. Je m'**en pourlèche les badigoinces** d'avance.
6. Deux cents **balles** pour du **brouille-ménage**?
7. La **boustifaille** à ce resto, ça doit être le **coup de fusil**!
8. C'est moi qui **régale**.

Leçon Trois

On a Piqué Ma Téloche!
(Someone swiped my television!)

[Using reductions, as heard on the audiotape]

1. T'as l'air **lessivé**.
2. J'vais aller au **plumard**.
3. J'ai entendu un **mec** qui **s'baladait** à l'extérieur de la **baraque** à côté d'chez moi.
4. Y pouvait pas **encarrer** par la **lourde**
5. L'a **bousillé** la f'nêt', lui.
6. Quel **bordel**!
7. J'vais appeler la **flicaille**
8. Le mec, y **s'est carapaté**.

[As you would see it written]

1. Tu as l'air **lessivé**.
2. Je vais aller au **plumard**.
3. J'ai entendu un **mec** qui **se baladait** à l'extérieur de la **baraque** à côté de chez moi.
4. Il ne pouvait pas **encarrer** par la **lourde**
5. Il a **bousillé** la fenêtre, lui.
6. Quel **bordel**!
7. Je vais appeler la **flicaille**
8. Le mec **s'est carapaté**.

Leçon Quatre

La Joie d'Être Bouchon

(The joy of being the youngest)

[Using reductions, as heard on the audiotape]

1. J'm'**en suis payé une tranche** à la soirée.
2. Ma **vieille** et mon **vieux**, y s'sont **bagarrés**.
3. Y s'sont **bouffé l'nez** mes **vieux**.
4. Ma **frangine**, è **s'est engueulée** avec mon **beauf**.
5. Leur **fiston** et leur **fifille**, y faisaient qu'**chialer**.
6. Mon **frangin**, y veut pas d'**moutards**.
7. **C'était pas ses oignons**!
8. Mon **beau-dab**, l'a **fait la gueule** toute la soirée!

[As you would see it written]

1. Je m'**en suis payé une tranche** à la soirée.
2. Ma **vieille** et mon **vieux** se sont **bagarrés**.
3. Ils se sont **bouffé le nez** mes **vieux**.
4. Ma **frangine s'est engueulée** avec mon **beauf**.
5. Leur **fiston** et leur **fifille** ne faisaient que **chialer**.
6. Mon **frangin** ne veut pas de **moutards**.
7. **Ce n'était pas ses oignons**!
8. Mon **beau-dab** a **fait la gueule** toute la soirée!

Leçon Cinq

Le Grande Boum
(The big bash)

[Using reductions, as heard on the audiotape]

1. C'est **chouette**, c'te **boum**!
2. **Mate** un peu comme y sont tous bien **fringués**.
3. Pourquoi tu **t'fais d'la bile**?
4. C'te **nana**-là, è m'**bigle**!
5. J'**en pince pour elle**.
6. J'vais la **brancher**.
7. T'es pas v'nu pour **draguer**?
8. J'ai envie d'**m'humecter les amygdales**.

[As you would see it written]

1. C'est **chouette**, cette **boum**!
2. **Mate** un peu comme ils sont tous bien **fringués**.
3. Pourquoi tu **te fais de la bile**?
4. Cette **nana**-là me **bigle**!
5. J'**en pince pour elle**.
6. Je vais la **brancher**.
7. Tu n'es pas venu pour **draguer**?
8. J'ai envie de **m'humecter les amygdales**.

Leçon Six

Le Chouchou du Prof

(The teacher's pet)

[Using reductions, as heard on the audiotape]

1. Le **prof**, y nous **fiche** toujours un **paquet** d'devoirs.
2. J'dois **bosser** c'soir.
3. J'vais **sécher l'cours** demain.
4. Je m'suis **fait étendre** à l'**exam**.
5. J'dois **potasser** mon français c'soir.
6. Y doit êt' **cinglé** d'penser qu'on peut lire tous ces **bouquins** en deux jours!
7. J'suis pas **calé** en **maths**.
8. Y m'**casse les pieds**, lui!

[As you would see it written]

1. Le **prof** nous **fiche** toujours un **paquet** de devoirs.
2. Je dois **bosser** ce soir.
3. Je vais **sécher le cours** demain.
4. Je me suis **fait étendre** à l'**exam**.
5. Je dois **potasser** mon français ce soir.
6. Il doit être **cinglé** de penser qu'on peut lire tous ces **bouquins** en deux jours!
7. Je ne suis pas **calé** en **maths**.
8. Il me **casse les pieds**, lui!

Leçon Sept

La Vie de Cossard
(The life of a lazy bum)

[Using reductions, as heard on the audiotape]

1. J'aurai du mal à **reprend' le collier** après mes vacances.
2. J'ai **enfilé des perles** pendant un mois.
3. Quand j'suis en vacances, j'**en fiche pas une rame**.
4. Y commence à m'**taper sur les nerfs**.
5. J'préfère passer mon temps à **lézarder**.
6. Qu'est-ce qu'y peut êt' **collant**!
7. J'dois **m'éclipser.**
8. C'est du **gâteau**!

[As you would see it written]

1. J'aurai du mal à **reprendre le collier** après mes vacances.
2. J'ai **enfilé des perles** pendant un mois.
3. Quand je suis en vacances, je n'**en fiche pas une rame**.
4. Il commence à me **taper sur les nerfs**.
5. Je préfère passer mon temps à **lézarder**.
6. Qu'est-ce qu'il peut être **collant**!
7. Je dois **m'éclipser.**
8. C'est du **gâteau**!

Leçon Huit

Dans le Zinc
(In the airplane)

[Using reductions, as heard on the audiotape]

1. J'espère que t'as pas eu à **poireauter** longtemps.
2. **Ça carbure**?
3. Tu vas pas croire ma **déveine**.
4. J'ai **paumé** mon billet d'avion.
5. Enfin, j'l'ai **déniché** après avoir **farfouillé** dans tous mes **bagos**.
6. J'ai dû **m'magner l'derche** pasque mon avion, l'allait **s'barrer**.
7. T'es **arrivée** à **faire dodo** dans l'**zinc**?
8. Quel **moulin à paroles**!

[As you would see it written]

1. J'espère que tu n'as pas eu à **poireauter** longtemps.
2. **Ça carbure**?
3. Tu ne vas pas croire ma **déveine**.
4. J'ai **paumé** mon billet d'avion.
5. Enfin, je l'ai **déniché** après avoir **farfouillé** dans tous mes **bagos**.
6. J'ai dû **me magner le derche** parce que mon avion allait **se barrer**.
7. Tu es **arrivée** à **faire dodo** dans le **zinc**?
8. Quel **moulin à paroles**!

Leçon Neuf

Un Coup de Fil

(A telephone call)

[Using reductions, as heard on the audiotape]

1. J'**en ai soupé** d'ses **bobards**!
2. Elle a **dégoisé** pendant toute une heure.
3. Quelle **crâneuse**!
4. J'**m'en fiche comme de ma première chaussette**.
5. Elle a pas la **bosse** du chant.
6. C'est pas **dans ses cordes**.
7. Sa **tignasse**, l'est horrible!
8. C'te nana, l'a un gros **pif** qui bouffe toute sa **tronche peinturlurée**.

[As you would see it written]

1. J'**en ai soupé** de ses **bobards**!
2. Elle a **dégoisé** pendant toute une heure.
3. Quelle **crâneuse**!
4. Je **m'en fiche comme de ma première chaussette**.
5. Elle n'a pas la **bosse** du chant.
6. Ce n'est pas **dans ses cordes**.
7. Sa **tignasse** est horrible!
8. Cette nana a un gros **pif** qui bouffe toute sa **tronche peinturlurée**.

Leçon Dix

J'ai la Crève!
(I'm sick!)

[Using reductions, as heard on the audiotape]

1. David, y dit qu'il a **attrapé la crève**.
2. Pauv' type. L'est très **mal fichu**.
3. Y s'croit toujours **à l'article de la mort**.
4. Les médecins, y **prennent la tangente** quand y l'voient **débarquer**.
5. L'hôpital, y doit avoir un **pageot** permanent pour lui avec son **blaze** dessus.
6. Y va **flipper** au point où y va s'faire une **belle corbuche**.
7. **Un d'ces quat'**, un **tranche-lard** y va lui dire de **passer su'l'billard**.
8. J'suis sûre qu'y s'ra **r'quinqué** et **en moins d'deux**!

[As you would see it written]

1. David dit qu'il a **attrapé la crève**.
2. Pauvre type. Il est très **mal fichu**.
3. Il se croit toujours **à l'article de la mort**.
4. Les médecins **prennent la tangente** quand ils le voient **débarquer**.
5. L'hôpital doit avoir un **pageot** permanent pour lui avec son **blaze** dessus.
6. Il va **flipper** au point où il va se faire une **belle corbuche**.
7. **Un de ces quatre**, un **tranche-lard** va lui dire de **passer sur le billard**.
8. Je suis sûre qu'il sera **requinqué** et **en moins de deux**!

Glossary

-A-

à deux doigts de (être)
See page: 157

à l'article de la mort (être)
See page: 193

agrafer (se faire)
See page: 47

aller en eau de boudin
See page: 5

apéro
See page: 27

arnaquer
See page: 135

arriver à faire quelque chose
See page: 157

attraper la crève
See page: 193

-B-

bagarrer (se)
See page: 69

bagos
See page: 157

balader (se)
See page: 47

balancer
See page: 136

balle
See page: 27

baraque
See page: 48

baratin
See page: 158

barman
See page: 27

barrer (se)
See page: 158

battant
See page: 193

beau-dab
See page: 69

beauf
See page: 69

belle-doche
See page: 70

belle/beau
See page: 194

bien roulé(e) (être)
See page: 175

bigler
See page: 91

blairer quelqu'un (ne pas pouvoir)
See page: 115

blaze
See page: 194

bordel
See page: 48

bosser
See page: 115

bosse de quelque chose (avoir la)
See page: 175

bouchon
See page: 70

boudin
See page: 175

bouffe
See page: 5

bouffer le nez (se)
See page: 70

bougeotte (avoir la)
See page: 136

boui-boui
See page: 28

boum
See page: 91

bouquin
See page: 116

bourré(e) (être)
See page: 28

bousiller
See page: 49

boustifaille
See page: 28

brancher
See page: 91

brouille-ménage
See page: 29

-C-

"Ça ne tourne pas rond"
See page: 194

"Ça saute aux yeux"
See page: 176

cailler
See page: 5

calé(e) en quelque chose (être)
See page: 116

carapater (se)
See page: 49

carburer
See page: 158

carrément
See page: 6

casseur
See page: 49

casser la gueule (se)
See page: 158

casser les oreilles à quelqu'un
See page: 159

casser les pieds à quelqu'un
See page: 117

"Ce n'est pas tes oignons"
See page: 70

"Chapeau!"
See page: 136

charrier
See page: 159

chialer
See page: 71

chocottes
See page: 176

chouchou(te)
See page: 117

chouette
See page: 91

cinglé(e) (être)
See page: 117

-D-

-E-

écliper (s')
See page: 138

écoper
See page: 50

en moins de deux
See page: 195

encarrer
See page: 50

enfiler des perles
See page: 139

engueuler
See page: 71

éponges
See page: 195

et patati et patata
See page: 177

étendre (se faire)
See page: 118

exact
See page: 50

exam
See page: 118

-F-

faire de la bile (se)
See page: 92

faire la gueule
See page: 72

faire le/la
See page: 72

farfouiller
See page: 160

fauché(e) (être)
See page: 139

fiche
See page: 118

fiche comme de sa première chaussette (s'en)
See page: 178

fiche une rame (ne pas en)
See page: 139

fifille
See page: 72

filer
See page: 30

fiston
See page: 72

flicaille
See page: 51

flipper
See page: 195

flotter
See page: 7

fourrer
See page: 51

frangine
See page: 73

frangin
See page: 73

fric
See page: 7

fringué(e) (être mal/bien)
See page: 93

frit(e) (être)
See page: 119

-G-

galerie
See page: 119

gargue
See page: 93

-H-

-I-

-J-

-L-

-M-

mettre au clou
See page: 52

moche à caler des roues de corbillard (être)
See page: 121

moulin à paroles
See page: 161

moutards
See page: 73

-N-

nana
See page: 95

nickel
See page: 30

-P-

pageot
See page: 196

paquet
See page: 122

passer sur le billard
See page: 196

paumer
See page: 162

payer une tranche (s'en)
See page: 73

peinturlurer
See page: 178

perdre la boule
See page: 96

piaf
See page: 9

picoler
See page: 31

pige
See page: 52

pince
See page: 96

pincer pour quelqu'un (en)
See page: 96

pioncer
See page: 140

piquer
See page: 53

placard
See page: 53

plancher
See page: 122

planquer
See page: 53

plombe
See page: 141

plumard
See page: 53

pognon
See page: 141

pointer (se)
See page: 31

poireauter
See page: 162

poivrot
See page: 31

potache
See page: 122

potasser
See page: 123

pourlécher les badigoinces (s'en)
See page: 32

première (de)
See page: 32

-U-

-V-

-Z-

ORDER FORM ON BACK

Prices subject to change

SPANISH	BOOK	CASSETTE
STREET SPANISH 1 *The Best of Spanish Slang*	$15.95	$12.50
STREET SPANISH 2 *The Best of Spanish Idioms (available '98)*	$15.95	$12.50
STREET SPANISH 3 *The Best of Naughty Spanish (available '98)*	$15.95	$12.50
STREET SPANISH SLANG DICTIONARY *(available '98)*	$16.95	

FRENCH	BOOK	CASSETTE
STREET FRENCH 1 *The Best of French Slang*	$15.95	$12.50
STREET FRENCH 2 *The Best of French Idioms*	$15.95	$12.50
STREET FRENCH 3 *The Best of Naughty French*	$15.95	$12.50
STREET FRENCH SLANG DICTIONARY & THESAURUS	$16.95	

AMERICAN-ENGLISH	BOOK	CASSETTE
STREET TALK 1 *How to Speak & Understand American Slang*	$16.95	$12.50
STREET TALK 2 *Slang Used in Popular American TV Shows*	$16.95	$12.50
STREET TALK 3 *The Best of American Idioms*	$18.95	$12.50
BIZ TALK 1 *American Business Slang & Jargon*	$16.95	$12.50
BIZ TALK 2 *More American Business Slang & Jargon*	$16.95	$12.50
BLEEP! *A Guide to Popular American Obscenities*	$14.95	$12.50

GERMAN	BOOK	CASSETTE
STREET GERMAN 1 *The Best of German Idioms*	$16.95	$12.50

P.O. Box 519 • Fulton, CA 95439 • USA

TOLL FREE Telephone/FAX (US/Canada):
1-888-4-ESLBOOKS (1-888-437-2665)

International orders Telephone/FAX line:
707-546-8878

ORDER FORM

Name ______________________________

(School/Company) ______________________________

Street Address ______________________________

City ____________ State/Province ____________ Postal Code ____________

Country ____________ Phone ____________

Quantity	Title	Book or Cassette?	Price Each	Total Price

Total for Merchandise	
Sales Tax (California Residents Only)	
Shipping (See Below)	
ORDER TOTAL	

METHOD OF PAYMENT (check one)

☐ Check or Money Order ☐ VISA ☐ Master Card ☐ American Express ☐ Discover

(Money orders and personal checks must be in U.S. funds and drawn on a U.S. bank.)

Credit Card Number: ______________________________ Card Expires: ____ ____

Signature *(important!)* →

SHIPPING

Domestic Orders: SURFACE MAIL (delivery time 5-7 days).
Add $4 shipping/handling for the first item · $1 for each additional item.
RUSH SERVICE available at extra charge.

International Orders: OVERSEAS SURFACE (delivery time 6-8 weeks).
Add $5 shipping/handling for the first item · $2 for each additional item.
OVERSEAS AIRMAIL available at extra charge.